THE CHANGEMAKER ATTITUDE

THE CHANGEMAKER ATTITUDE

WHY INDIVIDUALS MATTER IN THE FIGHT AGAINST CLIMATE CHANGE

JORDAN FOX

NEW DEGREE PRESS

THE CHANGEMAKER ATTITUDE
Why Individuals Matter in the Fight Against Climate Change

ISBN   978-1-64137-946-5   *Paperback*

           978-1-64137-756-0   *Kindle Ebook*

           978-1-64137-757-7   *Ebook*

*To my mom for showing me how amazing the world
is and for instilling in me the need to see it.*

To my dad for teaching me that everything is what you make of it.

To Debra Demske for the book she never finished.

And lastly, to the changemakers everywhere.

CONTENTS

SURVIVING MUDSLIDES

———

WHAT PEOPLE GET WRONG ABOUT CLIMATE CHANGE

Twenty months ago, Alhaji Siraj Bah was living on the streets of Sierra Leone with twenty dollars to his name. Today, he is the CEO and founder of Rusgal Trading, a company that uses coconut shells to create handcrafted bags and briquettes. The biodegradable bags replace plastic ones and the briquettes provide an alternative to burning firewood and charcoal, two of the leading causes of deforestation. These days, Bah sits between world leaders in climate change discussions and has been to the United Nations.

Stories like Bah's remind me that while we all tell ourselves we are too young or don't have the time to tackle global challenges like climate change, the truth is we can all make an impact if we set our minds to it. We say we'll wait until we have more money, connections, or stability, but the truth is there is no better time than the present.

Born in the Eastern Providence of Sierra Leone, Bah attended school until age thirteen when his father passed away and his mother was no longer able to care for him or pay for his schooling. He then moved to Freetown to search for a better life and began picking up odd jobs, like cleaning houses and fetching water.

For four years, Bah continued to search for ways to make money. Meanwhile, he was homeless, sleeping on bridges, on tables, and in abandoned cars.

"Nobody wants to sleep on the street. It's so hard. Just imagine: During winter, you're sleeping outside. Even though it does not snow here in Africa, it's so cold. I slept on the street for, like, four years. Could you imagine? It's so hard for me to see somebody on the street. I get very emotional," Bah recollects now.

He found his first stroke of luck when his friend's mother allowed him to live with her already-crowded family in exchange for help with jobs around the house. He began working at a water factory making one dollar a day and saving up enough to send back to his sick mother. He was beginning to make a life for himself when tragedy struck again.

In 2017, a devastating landslide destroyed Sierra Leone and killed everyone in his adoptive family, leaving the eighteen-year-old to fend for himself once again. The CEO at the water factory allowed him to sleep on the floor and he spent his days there, alternating between sleeping and working.

You'd think this utter lack of resources would destroy someone's entrepreneurial spirit. According to most psychologists, you need the basic building blocks—food, water, and shelter—before you can even contemplate other goals in life. But that didn't stop Bah.

He began researching the causes of the landslide that killed his friends and quickly learned the heavy rains were aggravated by deforestation and plastic filling up the gutters. It takes plastic bags around 500 years to decompose and, even then, they only decompose enough to break into microplastics that continue to pollute the environment. Paper bags, on the other hand, take less than three months to degrade.

In January 2018, Bah went to the market and bought paper, which he then crafted into bags. The plan was to sell customized bags to individuals and businesses. He didn't have a background in design or engineering, but he did have passion, drive, and some YouTube videos.

"So, I needed to stand up for these people. I never wanted anything like this to happen anymore, so I needed to be a changemaker. I wanted to do something, and even though I had nothing back then, I wanted to do something. I needed to do something. Money should not stop me. Money should not be something that stopped me from being a changemaker," Bah said.

Despite his determined mindset, many obstacles still stood in his way. Twenty dollars could only get him so far and he struggled to get enough money for supplies. Without equipment like a printer, it took six hours for the customized bags to fully dry. He also didn't have any companies to model his after, and with very little focus on environmental issues in Sierra Leone, funding was difficult to secure.

About a month into his new enterprise, Bah received an order from a hotel for one thousand bags. After a few moments relishing in the victory, he realized he only had ten days to finish the order. At the time, he was working alone. For one week, he worked sixteen hours a day to craft and print the bags. When he delivered the products on time, even the hotel was impressed. It was his first test and Bah had proved he could create and deliver a product on time without any assistance. It was this small victory that gave him the confidence to continue working and dreaming bigger.

He says he used to look at Facebook for inspirational stories but now he just compares his present life to what it was one year ago. With all that he has accomplished, new challenges do not faze him.

"There is nothing bigger than me anymore because I did it with nothing. So why not now when I have something?" Bah said.

Just two months later, he used the money from his big order to create briquettes—usually made from coal or wood—out of coconut husks, creating a smokeless, odorless, affordable alternative that didn't cut down trees. By November, he finally saved enough money to buy a printing machine. A month later, Rugsal Trading began donating 40 percent of its revenue to orphans and poor students. As soon as he was able to get a place of his own, Bah took in all the kids he had known from the streets, giving them jobs and a place to live.

By February 2019, he began making the paper bags from banana fibers in an effort to continue reducing the impact of Rugsal Trading. Today, Rusgal Trading has produced more than 250,000 eco-friendly bags, 120 tons of clean and smokeless briquettes, and saved 15,000 trees, all while providing Bah's community with affordable fuel. He has managed to turn twenty dollars into a company with eighty-eight employees that is growing every day. He believes his dream is never big enough.

"Twenty months ago, I was a street boy. Now [I'm] a boy with no degree who sits between world leaders."

If he had procrastinated and waited until he was more secure, he would never have made it to where he is now. He has now saved enough money to buy a flat and move his mom to the city.

His advice is simple: "Use what you have, do what you can, and do it now."

No matter how many times I hear Bah's incredible story, I am struck by how logical his response was to overwhelming tragedy. Over 1,000 people died in the 2017 mudslide, leaving an additional 3,000 people, including Bah, homeless.

He told me things like, "I had to fight to combat deforestation, air pollution, and waste management because I never wanted anybody to experience what I experienced." Despite the widespread suffering felt by many afterward, he felt personally responsible for combating the issue. This sense of responsibility is very rare in tragedies in which so many people are affected and there is no single entity to blame.

Despite the countless moments when he could have given up, he never did. He remained focused on the impact he could have on his community and that inspires me.

Every day, we are inundated with news about our impending doom: the massive, irreparable damage we have caused our planet that we are now starting to see play out in real time. Since 1972, the sea levels have risen about 14 millimeters and half of that has occurred in the last eight years. By 2100, it's possible they will rise by a meter, which would displace 10 percent of the world's population.[1] We constantly hear about the grim future of our world after a 1.5-to-2-degree temperature rise. Among many other scary scenarios, this would destroy up to 40 percent of the Amazon rainforest, which would, in turn, release more carbon.[2] This isn't a problem we can ignore for the sake of the economy either, as the National Bureau of Economic Research has estimated. Continuing on this path will reduce the world's real GDP by 7.22 percent by the year 2100.[3] Alternately, the global economy stands to gain between $126.68 trillion and $616.12 trillion by 2100 if nations can reduce greenhouse gas emissions to an optimal level.[4]

As individuals, we cannot even contemplate the scope of this problem. In fact, these numbers mean almost nothing to me.

---

1   Sky News Staff, "What Will Happen As The World Gets Warmer?" *Sky News,* October 8, 2018.

2   Ibid.

3   Matthew E. Kahn et al., "Long-Term Macroeconomic Effects of Climate Change: A Cross-Country Analysis," *The National Bureau of Economic Research*, NBER Working Paper No. 26167 (2019).

4   Yi-Ming Wei et al., "Self-preservation strategy for approaching global warming targets in the post-Paris Agreement era," *Nature Communications*, 11, 1624 (2020): 1-4.

I have no clue what a 14-millimeter rise in global sea levels or 40 percent of the Amazon rainforest looks like. It just sounds overwhelmingly bad. Based on these painful facts, it is easy to see why people feel so powerless. Growing up among these horrible realizations, I have had my fair share of powerless moments.

Like any person encountering what seems like an insurmountable loss, I have faced what I can only describe as the five stages of grief. First, denial. *Humans have been wrong before. Obviously, the entire planet isn't going to go down in flames in my lifetime, right? I mean, at one point in history, we thought the earth was flat.*

I spent most of my life in complete denial, telling myself that since I was young, someone else would fix it because this was a job for adults. When I saw news of melting ice caps, I would remind myself how far away that was and how it wasn't really affecting me.

Next came the anger. *How dare past generations leave us in this situation and expect us to figure it out while we are still so young? How can these companies get away with polluting the earth with absolutely no repercussions?* I internally bargained, telling myself I would use less and clean up more if it would just go away.

I grew up in the mountains of Colorado, where environmental issues present a direct threat to the livelihood of our ski town. We were taught to leave no trace on our frequent hiking and camping trips, and I am incredibly lucky to feel so connected to the earth.

I always believed I could have an impact until I learned just one hundred companies are responsible for 71 percent of global emissions since 1988.[5] Even worse, just twenty-five of those companies were responsible for more than half of the global industrial emissions.[6] After learning this, I began to lose faith in mankind and our ability to solve problems.

It was in the fourth stage of grief, depression, when I let myself succumb to a doomsday vision of the end of the world as we know it.

Even in those moments, I struggled to accept that individual actions didn't matter. Sitting around and waiting for the big polluters to stop didn't seem like an option. But at the same time, I couldn't help but wonder if my recycling and conservation efforts were pointless.

In my desperate curiosity, I began looking for people who were making real, tangible change and found a world of innovators making a difference in their communities. It wasn't until I found their stories that I was able to accept the state of our world and actually feel optimistic about our future.

I began interviewing young eco-innovators with the hope of understanding what was different about them that allowed them to accomplish so much. At first glance, these innovators from around the world had very little in common. But the more people I interviewed, the more I began to understand they all share a common mindset: a

5   Paul Griffin, "CDP Carbon Majors Report 2017," The Carbon Majors Database, CDP, July 2017.

6   Ibid.

passion and a positivity that forced them beyond fear and obstacles. What I've realized is there is an attitude they all share, one we can all learn from—and one that has given me hope for the future.

Even now, I struggle to find balance between productive individual action and meaningless displays of token environmentalism. On one hand, we spend so much of our time worried about minute things. We have big debates over small pieces of the puzzle, trivializing large issues like plastic pollution until we are yelling about the structural integrity of a paper versus a plastic straw. Focusing on the smallest personal choices distracts us from the bigger, more structural issues occurring around the world. On the other hand, the belief that you have no power in the world creates a destructive pessimism that leads to inaction.

Here is where we get lost. We desperately want to take action and fix the problem, but we can't seem to find the middle ground. Tweeting about straws is easy yet has very little impact on the world.

As Edmund Burke said, "The only thing necessary for the triumph of evil is for good men to do nothing." So where exactly is this sweet spot between ignoring the problem and spending all of our energy on unimportant things? Like in the tale of Goldilocks, we are trying to find the porridge that is just right.

This sweet spot doesn't have to mean starting your own eco-business, although I hope to dispel the myth of it being too difficult for people to undertake. Instead, this sweet spot is about using what you can to make a tangible difference without wasting time and energy on meaningless actions.

Many people believe that in this global fight against climate change, individuals and their actions don't make a difference. But those people aren't paying enough attention to our secret weapon: each other. Our obsession with numbers and data have led us to overestimate the power of processes and underestimate the power of individuals, and that has been our biggest mistake.

Through this process, I've talked to young people around the world who are doing incredible things. If I've learned anything, it's that individual people do matter. They have the ability to make changes in their local communities, inspiring others to take action as well. Their commitment and perseverance have proven to me that while humans are part of the problem, they are also our much-needed solution.

A study entitled "How Hope and Doubt Affect Climate Change Mobilization" found that of Americans who accept global warming is happening, many can't name reasons to be hopeful.[7] In addition to being flat-out depressing, this is dangerous. Without hope, there is no need for individuals to respond and make changes. The same study warned against blind hope, arguing that a combination of both hope and practicality is needed to create action.[8]

---

7   Jennifer R. Marlon et al., "How Hope and Doubt Affect Climate Change Mobilization," *Frontiers in Communication*, 4, 2297 (2019): 1-5.

8   Ibid.

This book makes the case for a new mindset to tackle our environmental issues because, for many reasons, what we are doing right now is just not working. For everyone who has ever worried about the future, felt powerless to the bigger forces that make decisions for the rest of us, or ignored negative environmental news because it all seemed hopeless, this book will change your outlook as well as show you the right way to take action.

Since starting this process, I no longer feel as afraid about our future. I finally reached the last stage of grief: acceptance and hope. I am deeply optimistic about our future because I've seen the power humans can have on their environment and in their community.

As famous cognitive psychologist Amos Tversky put it, "As a pessimist, you suffer twice." I am an optimist, not because I think we have it all figured out, but because I see no other way of proceeding forward than with positivity, hope, and pure determination.

After all, pessimism signals inaction and we don't have time to wallow.

CHAPTER 1

THE CONTROLLED MELTDOWN

HOW TO OVERCOME INITIAL FEAR

My sixth-grade teachers loved to tell us, *"Life sucks and then you die."* If it seems like an aggressive thing to tell a bunch of eleven-year olds, it's because it is. That year, my class of sixty kids was split-taught by two teachers who, most likely fed up dealing with sixty eleven-year-olds, began implementing group activities to teach us about the world.

In the first activity, they told us we were responsible for a village and needed five fish to feed our people. The middle of the room was filled with Swedish Fish candy. There were no other rules—just rounds representing years, during which we all had a certain amount of time to "fish." Unsurprisingly, the minute we were set free in the "ocean," all considerations for the needs of others disappeared. Somewhere around the third "year," each of us hoarded mounds of Swedish Fish and none remained in the middle.

Some kids ended up with piles of candy while others only had a few pieces because, of course, life is not fair. The game was a reflection of the tragedy of the commons, the idea that individuals acting according to their own self-interests depletes common resources.[9] When the sugar high and chaos dissipated, we were able to see the error of our ways. It was in those first moments I understood what we were doing to the world. It wasn't a result of bad people making bad choices; it was just a result of bad incentives. The game was not framed for us to holistically balance our needs against that of the environment; we were just told to feed our villages and that is what we did. Reflecting on the game, it is pretty obvious with the instructions presented that the ocean would quickly run out of fish and we would not be able to provide for all our villages. But the students never took this thought into account.

That's when a world beyond my classroom, city, and country began to develop in my mind. It is also when the panic began to set in. *Was the world going to end? If we couldn't keep our hands off the Swedish Fish, how could anyone else be expected to?* I'm sure anyone who has contemplated this issue for more than a few minutes experiences the same panic. It likely involves lots of sweating and a pit in the bottom of your stomach so large you feel as though it could swallow you.

As scary as it is, you are not alone. In America, 69 percent of people say they are at least "somewhat worried" about global

9   Garrett Hardin, "Tragedy of the Commons," The Library of Economics and Liberty, Accessed April 30, 2020.

warming with 29 percent saying they are "very worried," according to the most recent study by the Yale Program on Climate Communication.[10] Americans feel many emotions surrounding our current global crisis, with 53 percent feeling "disgusted," 51 percent feeling "helpless," and the majority believing their families (56 percent), their communities (57 percent), the world's poor (65 percent), or future generations (75 percent) will be affected.[11]

Even professionals who try to solve this problem struggle with the gravity of it.

Jay Koh is the current managing director and founder of Lightsmith Group, a global investment platform that focuses on climate resilience and adaptation. In 2014, he was named to the Private Sector Advisory Group of the United Nations Green Climate Fund as part of an effort to mobilize the private sector to deal with climate change. We all focus on innovations to change the future but rarely think about the other half of the problem: adaptation. When Koh was tasked to provide the board with advice on adaptation, he remarked it was the first time he had even heard the word in reference to climate change.

Adaptation is an overwhelming task because, even as the rest of the world scrambles to stop these terrifying effects, someone has to solve our immediate problems, like the prevalent fires in California, childhood asthma, hurricanes, and droughts.

---

10   Anthony Leiserowitz et al., "Climate Change in the American Mind: December 2018," January 22, 2019.

11   Ibid.

Koh began thinking about this problem in terms of a private investment strategy, which is usually a ten-year plan. It was in those moments he thought about the gravity of the situation. He was forty-eight at the time and his daughter was two years old, so the end of the ten years would mark a significantly different place in their lives.

> *"What you then suddenly realize is the one thing you have a fair amount of certainty now, if you believe the science, is that the world will look fairly different than it does right now, from a climate change perspective. The frequency and severity of these types of events will be increased. Hurricane cycles are roughly, three to four-year cycles. You're guaranteed at least two, two and a half of these within ten years, and they're not going to be better than the last cycles. Cape Town ran out of water last year, Chennai ran out of water this year. How many more of those will have happened by the end of ten years?"*

As Koh discovered, once you start envisioning this future, your decision making, urgency, and choices—both personal and professional—will be very different.

In 2014, Jay was asked to contemplate this important issue as a member of the Private Sector Advisory Group of the UN Green Climate Fund and propose solutions. As scary as climate change is in a vague, abstract way, the thought exercise of imagining his daughter's future fueled his choices. The younger you are now, the scarier this exercise often is: What will the world look like in five, ten, fifteen years? But we cannot let the fear stop us there.

Contemplating the future with regard to climate insta-bility is so stressful that professionals had to create a new word: eco-anxiety. Eco-anxiety describes the "worry or agitation caused by concerns about the pres-ent and future state of the environment."[12] According to one of the authors of an American Psychological Association guide to mental health and our changing climate, the psychological responses to climate change include conflict avoidance, fatalism, fear, helplessness, and resignation. These responses are "keeping us, and our nation, from properly addressing the core causes of and solutions for our changing climate and from build-ing and supporting psychological resiliency."[13] Eco-anx-iety is part of the paralysis stopping people from action, which is why it is so essential we move past it. Michael Apathy, a psychotherapist in New Zealand, said, "The impulse to do something proactive is very, very healthy, in my mind," a statement that seems contrary to his surname.[14] "But when that becomes over-relied on as a substitute for facing the fear and deep rage and loss periodically, we get uncreative and disillusioned and backed up against a wall."[15]

So how do we hold these two ideas in our head at the same time in a way that is actually productive?

12 Jennifer Huizen, "What to know about eco-anxiety," Medical News Today, December 19, 2019.
13 Susan Clayton et al., "MENTAL HEALTH AND OUR CHANGING CLI-MATE: IMPACTS, IMPLICATIONS, AND GUIDANCE," March 2017.
14 Eve Andrews, "Climate anxiety doesn't have to ruin your life. Here's how to manage it," Grist, September 5, 2017.
15 Ibid.

As Koh said, "Between those two things is sort of a path towards actual forward movement which is: You need to accept that this is an incredibly urgent, potentially catastrophic existential problem, and accept the seriousness and the urgency of that and then move through that. Then, try to take practical action and think about how to make it a tractable problem from a practical and pragmatic perspective."

So next time you want to panic, remember it's not the panic that matters but what comes next: taking action.

I recently saw a video on Facebook about Beth Fairchild, a woman diagnosed with terminal cancer at age thirty-four and told she had two years to live.[16] She had to go through the unthinkable process of telling her young kids about her bleak and terrifying situation. She told the interviewer, "I saw the fear in their eyes. Mommy couldn't assure them things would be okay, but I could show them I wasn't going to give up."[17]

As Fairchild said in the video, "Every day is a good day, even the bad days because if you are feeling joy or happiness or amusement or even when you are sad and frightened, those are all feelings, and they are all things you should find gratitude for experiencing. Even on the days I feel hurt, I'm glad I'm here to experience it."[18]

---

16   Style Like U, "How Terminal Cancer Showed Beth Fairchild That She Was Enough," Facebook, October 2019.

17   Ibid.

18   Ibid.

She has channeled her fear and emotions into activism and said that every time she experiences a loss, it fuels her fire and pushes her to do more.[19]

When we are faced with fear, we have two options: give up or let it fuel our fires. Just because fear can be paralyzing doesn't mean it has to be. Knowledge is important for recognizing a problem but emotions are crucial for attacking it. According to three experiments conducted by psychologists at the University of Toronto, those who accept or embrace negative emotions show higher levels of psychological well-being and are better suited to cope with stress.[20]

As scary as it is to look into the uncertain future, Koh uses his "Marty McFly approach" from *Back to the Future* to understand how much change is possible.

> *"2009 was the depths of the financial crisis, and if you explain to anyone that you thought autonomous or electric vehicles would be almost inevitable and that the super majority of new electricity build on the planet earth would be solar and wind, people would have thought you were out of your mind, right? And that's where we are now. So it's not as if you can't shift the trajectory of the world by action, innovation, entrepreneurship, and optimism. All these kinds of human qualities that enable us to make progress."*

19   Ibid.
20   Brett Q. Ford et al., "The psychological health benefits of accepting negative emotions and thoughts: Laboratory, diary, and longitudinal evidence," *Journal of Personality and Social Psychology*, July 13, 2017.

Ten years from now, the world will look completely different but we have agency in shaping the outcome. Humankind has always faced problems. We just happen to be at the front of a very complicated one but that shouldn't make it any less approachable.

Even when Koh faced the overwhelming concept of adaptation to climate change, which is affecting people around the world in real time, he was able to put it in perspective. For his daughter and many others, it was imperative he keeps moving forward. Despite the pain of acknowledging the facts, he was able to recognize the human qualities like action and optimism that can spark changes within a society.

As my sixth-grade teachers consistently instilled in us, life is unfair. However, it does not mean we should accept it as an unchangeable fact that blinds us from action. Despite their unorthodox teaching methods and efforts to get us to recognize mass inequities and unfairness, my teachers somehow made me love the world more.

JUST REMEMBER:

1. Remind yourself of the amazing progress we have made as a society.

2. Move past the fear. You are not alone in being scared, but don't accept fear as an excuse for inaction.

3. Rather than looking at the problem as a whole, look local at small actions you can take.

CHAPTER 2

DON'T TELL ME IT'S A FREAKING STRAW

———

AVOIDING OUR CURRENT PITFALLS

In 2015, marine biologist Christine Figgerner posted a video of a turtle with a plastic straw stuck in its nose. It is a painful eight-minute video of her team slowly extracting the straw.[21] The turtle sneezes and struggles to get away as the researchers pull what they originally believe to be a worm out of its nose.[22] When the turtle starts to bleed, the researchers worry the plastic straw is touching the turtle's brain and cannot be removed.[23] They continue to reassure the pained turtle that it will be so much better once they are done.[24] Halfway

---

21 Sophia Rosenbaum, "She Recorded That Heartbreaking Turtle Video. Here's What She Wants Companies Like Starbucks to Know About Plastic Straws," *Time*, July 17, 2018.

22 Ibid.

23 Ibid.

24 Ibid.

through the video, the videographer exclaims, "Don't tell me it is a freaking straw!"[25]

One hundred and forty-seven thousand views on YouTube later, this simple video prompted a massive public outcry and plastic straws became the centerpiece of the environmental conversation. Activists used this momentum to convince people to change their habits over what they viewed as a highly visible piece of the plastic problem that consumers may be willing to go without. It was a stepping-stone to tackling plastic consumption. Figgerner told *Time* when asked about this new environmental endeavor birthed from her video, "I'm, of course, happy, but I don't want the corporations to feel like they're getting off easily just by eliminating plastic straws. I hope this is the first step."[26]

While cities like Seattle banned plastic straws completely (eventually followed by Washington, DC; Alameda, Berkeley, Manhattan Beach, and Oakland, CA; Monmouth Beach, NJ; and Fort Myers, FL), states like California compromised by requiring all sit-down restaurants only give out plastic straws to those who request them.[27] Companies like Alaska Airlines, Royal Caribbean Cruises, Ikea, A&W Canada, Starbucks, and many others raced to get ahead of the movement and eliminated or pledged to eliminate plastic straws from their operations.[28]

---

25   Ibid.
26   Ibid.
27   James Rainey, "How business groups are fighting a wave of anti-plastic straw laws," *NBC News*, March 1, 2019.
28   James Rainey, "'Banning plastic straws will not be enough': The fight to clean the oceans," *NBC News*, December 30, 2018.

"If our oceans are going to be filled with more plastic than fish in a couple of generations, isn't that something we should think about the next time we're reaching for that plastic straw wrapped in more plastic?" asked Katy Tang, the author of the legislation banning single-use plastic utensils in San Francisco. *"With the plastic bag ordinance, there were a lot of fears and anxiety and complaints about how we were going to comply with the ordinance, and then the composting ordinance came along, and everybody was also very anxious about it smelling up our garages. Now it's such a normal part of our lives."*[29]

Despite talk about the new movement spreading across social media with tags like #StopSucking, businesses, free enterprise groups, and disability advocates pushed back swiftly, pointing out many disabled people need plastic straws to drink.

Lawrence Carter-Long, the director of communications at the Disability Rights Education and Defense Fund, responded to the San Francisco ban by telling the Guardian, "What has happened here is a situation that happens time and time again when it comes to the disability community, and that is, 'Out of sight, out of mind.' If people don't personally need straws, they fail or neglect to realize that there are people that do."[30]

Paper straws have often been touted as the environmentally conscious alternative to plastic. However, they do not accommodate disabled people and are incredibly frustrating to use.

---

29 Vivian Ho, "'People need them': The trouble with the movement to ban plastic straws," *The Guardian*, August 25, 2018.

30 Ibid.

Sacha Haworth, the political director of American Bridge 21st Century, a liberal opposition research group, tweeted, "Paper straws are terrible. I want my milkshake to taste like milkshake and not disintegrated newspaper. @ me, I'm ready."[31]

Despite all the fighting about paper straws as a new plastic alternative, they are not good for the environment either. Their production emits more air pollution and greenhouse gases while killing trees that could absorb carbon dioxide. They also require more energy and water to make, don't degrade much faster than plastic, and are inefficient to recycle.[32] So, while paper straws may not choke a turtle, they still hurt the environment, just in different ways.

As a reminder, all this infighting pertains solely to one piece of plastic. How did we find ourselves having serious arguments over details as inconsequential to the climate conversation as the structural integrity of paper straws? How is this productive?

Elizabeth Warren said it well in a tweet after the Climate Town Hall. "The fossil fuel industry wants to keep us arguing about light bulbs and cheeseburgers, while 70 percent of pollution comes from just three industries. We need to focus on creating big, structural change to tackle this climate crisis and the Washington corruption head-on."[33]

---

31   Sacha Haworth, Twitter post, July 15, 2019, 11:39 a.m.
32   Jane Mcgrath, "Which is more environmentally friendly: paper or plastic?," How Stuff Works, August 20, 2008.
33   Elizabeth Warren, Twitter post, September 4, 2019, 8:58 p.m.

In our efforts to legitimize our own power as individuals, we have gotten stuck on where we should focus our energy. But in taking back our own power, instead of creating structural change, we have let those who are most responsible off the hook and have wasted valuable efforts infighting about what matters and what doesn't.

Rather than a serious conversation about plastic use, straws became both controversial and a joke. President Trump began selling ten packs of plastic straws for fifteen dollars with his name on the side.[34] His straws were a symbol, and he stated, "Much like most liberal ideas, paper straws don't work, and they fall apart instantly."[35] His campaign reportedly earned $670,000 from the merchandise.[36] Meanwhile, subsequent counteractions like glass "Trump Sucks" straws emerged.[37] Those companies deemed to be on the right side of the issue made lots of money but the only thing created was more division.

In cases like a recent fist fight between a customer and McDonald's worker that erupted after the customer was informed they only give out straws upon request, it is easy to see the underlying tension that has resulted from something so simple.[38]

---

34 Jessica Taylor, "Trump Seizes on Soggy Paper Straws as Campaign Issue: 'Make Straws Great Again,'" *NPR*, July 19, 2019.

35 Ibid.

36 Ibid.

37 PR Newswire, "Responding to Trump's Plastic Straws, Bernie Sanders Supporters Launch 'Trump Sucks' Metal Straws," *Market Insider*, August 5, 2019.

38 Christina Zdanowicz, "A man attacked a McDonald's employee over a straw and she fought back," *CNN*, January 4, 2019.

The issue isn't about whether we would be better off using less plastic. The problem lies in the controversy, pushback, and stalemate over a relatively minor issue. The national conversation about an environmental issue is great because this increases awareness, but it is hindered by its narrowness and the controversy surrounding it.

Every night at home, my parents designate one of the children to do the dishes. It usually ends up being whoever is closest to the kitchen when one of them realizes the kitchen is dirty after dinner. This prompts yelling about how unfair it is. "Jack is never down here for dinner, so he never has to clean up!" "Come on Dad, I have to finish this project, and Lauren is not doing anything!" Despite the protests, my parents always hold their ground and retreat to their room so they do not have to hear about it anymore. Occasionally, my dad will come back to remind us that "In all the time spent complaining, you could have finished cleaning."

In the same way yelling is an ineffective way to clean a kitchen, fighting is an ineffective way to lower our carbon footprint.

Our tendency to grasp onto these minute issues only creates more division, less action, and eventually hopelessness about progress. These are valiant battles. However, getting into Twitter fights about the merits of paper straws and desperately yelling about this issue as if it is the hill you have chosen to die on for the environment is emotionally draining and often void of real action.

The low-cost hypothesis of environmental behavior says people will engage in low-cost actions that have little impact over high-cost actions that would make a more meaning-ful difference.[39] Tweeting makes us feel involved but has an extremely minimal effect on the environment, yet we feel it is better than nothing. To some degree it is, but it is not the most efficient use of our power.

We get so caught up in this endless cycle of problems we've been told to get angry about that we become numb to big issues that should spark the same inflammatory outrage. Again, it is so much easier to get angry about straws than to address the structural issues causing climate change.

It just takes a moment to remove yourself from the noise and focus on a Goldilocks-type solution. One person yelling into the void does not change anything and neither does a million people tweeting about straws. It is in these moments that we have to pick our battles and begin to think about how to create the most change.

Focusing on plastic straws alone is unhelpful and addressing the whole problem is overwhelming. So where do we start?

According to Andreas Y. Gruson, the chairman and CEO of FleetGenius, LLC, and executive chairman of Compology, Inc., we have to address the root of the problem. Gruson has always been involved in the environmental services industry and grew up collecting scrap metals to sell to recyclers. Every year, he attends the premier sustainability conference hosted by Waste Management, Inc., during which attendees discuss some of the

---

39 Janet Swim et al., "Psychology and global climate change: Addressing a multi-faceted phenomenon and set of challenges." *American Psychological Association 66.* (August 2009) 241-250.

daunting environmental issues facing our world. Last year, they discussed plastics in the ocean and it quickly became apparent how difficult it is to remove plastic given the ocean's depth, expansiveness, and extreme conditions. Rather than committing resources to a less effective and expensive ocean expedition, they focused on the source of 90 percent of the waste in the oceans: rivers. By looking at the problem differently, they would be able to remove plastic before it feeds into the ocean in a much more hospitable environment. In environmental sustainability, Gruson does not believe you need to shoot for the moon.

"You just have to start and do something. Any action you take is significant. Small steps and changes lead to big impact. The best changes are usually evolutionary. Waiting for revolutionary changes often results in inaction and status quo."

* * *

Getting rid of plastic straws wouldn't even make a dent in the plastic pollution that ends up in our oceans. While consumers are more willing to make changes in that area, making it a good target for activists, we have forgotten it is only a small symbol of a larger issue. A 2017 study discovered that 46 percent of plastic waste in the Great Pacific Garbage Patch was made up of fishing nets and while plastic straws are among the top ten most common items found on beaches, they don't make up a great proportion of the waste. In fact, of the eight million tons of plastic that end up in oceans every year, plastic straws only make up 0.025 percent.[40]

---

40   James Rainey, "'Banning plastic straws will not be enough': The fight to clean the oceans," *NBC News*, December 30, 2018.

Like many other social media movements, the #StopSucking hashtag has increased momentum and attention, forcing governments and businesses to respond to these concerns.

During all the commotion about plastic straws, Starbucks announced that it plans to remove them from all 25,085 locations and replace them with lids that look like sippy cups.[41] It was a great public relations move that showed people their pressure, concerns, and tweets had created measurable change. But like many other promises, it fell short. Environmentalists were quick to point out the new lids would be made of more plastic than the straws.

Starbucks responded by saying it was still an improvement because "recycling systems can capture the lid versus the straw, which is too light and escapes into the waste stream."[42] But just because lids "can" be recycled doesn't mean they will, especially given that between 1950 and 2015, only 9.5 percent of plastic was recycled.[43]

This doesn't mean we should stop applying pressure; it just means we can't let it drain all our power and focus. The encouraging part is that people are paying attention and ready to get angry. We just need to direct that energy to the right outlets.

Meanwhile, cities are making progress by changing regulations to tackle plastic waste. More than 400 states and cities in the

41   Ibid.
42   Ibid.
43   Ibid.

US have banned or taxed plastic bags.[44] Seattle enacted a plastic bag ban and five-cent charge on paper bags in 2012.[45] San Francisco and several other local governments banned single-use plastic in 2007, with California following in 2014.[46] Chicago implemented a seven-cent tax on checkout bags in 2017.[47]

So why does this tend to work even as the fight rages on without an end in sight on the national stage and social media channels? In short, it's because it's local. Cities can act quicker to make changes based on the needs of their citizens. Big lobbyists and organizations aren't fighting as hard at the city level but ground-up work is how change happens. Once again, this reinforces the importance of individuals to change their communities.

Kate Icopini, the general manager at Portland bar and restaurant St. Jack, began encouraging other businesses to stop using straws after switching to a more eco-friendly option.[48] She has hosted bar crawls and dinner series raising money for the Surfrider Foundation, a nonprofit working to clean up oceans.[49]

On one such occasion, she spoke directly to others in her industry, "What we decided to do was get really loud about it and

44   Matthew Zeitlin, "Do plastic bag taxes or bans curb waste? 400 cities and states tried it out," *Vox Media*, August 27, 2019.

45   Seattle City Council, "Plastic Bag Ban," Seattle.gov, Accessed April 20, 2020.

46   Matthew Zeitlin, "Do plastic bag taxes or bans curb waste? 400 cities and states tried it out," *Vox Media*, August 27, 2019.

47   Ibid.

48   Brenna Houck, "Why the World Is Hating on Plastic Straws Right Now," *Eater*, July 12, 2018.

49   Ibid.

call on our peers in the industry to join us. I think a lot of restaurants...do the right thing both for the world and for their business. But like most things, you are stronger together."[50]

This is just one person running one restaurant in a town in Oregon, but she was successful because her voice and actions matter to the community. Change happens when people influence others to take action locally, focusing on the underlying issue without being petty or politicizing.

Benjamin Franklin once said, "Well done is better than well said."[51] There are so many ways people can take action in their own lives but simply shifting from talking about the issue to changing your own habits is a great start. When people tweet and yell about plastic straws, businesses feel pressure to change from using straws to plastic tops. But when a large enough group of people decide to cut their use of disposable plastics altogether, companies have to make changes that address the problem at large.

JUST REMEMBER:
1. Think global, act local. Look at the big picture, then find local solutions in your city that could make a difference.

2. Pick your battles. Don't waste your emotional energy arguing online. Use that energy to drive local initiatives instead.

---

50 Ibid.
51 Benjamin Franklin, "Poor Richard's Almanack, 1737," AMDOCS: DOCUMENTS FOR THE STUDY OF AMERICAN HISTORY, Accessed April 20, 2020.

3. Find your "biggest-bang-for-the-buck" action: What can you personally do that will empower you to continue improving rather than overwhelm you? Think planting trees locally or finding ways to amplify your voice.

CHAPTER 3

LIGHTING THE MATCH

WHY INDIVIDUAL
CHANGEMAKERS MATTER

History often forgets people like E.D. Morel, who began as a young shipping clerk working at Elder Demster Shipping during the 1890s.[52] At the time of Belgium's colonial rule over the area, Elder Demster Shipping was making a fortune transporting and selling rubber in the Congo.[53] Morel began noticing that while the ships leaving the Congo contained valuable products like rubber and ivory, the ships arriving there contained guns, explosives, and chains rather than any commercial goods.[54] Through his observations, he determined the supposed "free trade" between Europe and the Congo could not possibly exist.[55] As a result of these observations, he investigated further and uncovered the brutal

---

52 Adam Hochschild, *King Leopold's Ghost: A Story of Greed, Terror, and Heroism in Colonial Africa*, New York: Mariner Books, 1998.

53 Ibid.

54 Ibid.

55 Ibid.

crimes against humanity occurring in the Congo, including widespread slave labor, murder, torture, starvation, and other horrible cruelties.[56]

When Morel tried to confront those he worked for, they dismissed him and tried to buy his silence.[57] Rather than taking the money he clearly needed, he quit at a great expense to him and his family in order to expose these atrocities through journalism.[58] He feverishly pursued this goal and started his own magazine, the *West African Mail*. He published several pamphlets and a book entitled *Affairs of West Africa*.[59] Morel's work outraged much of the public in Europe and prompted further investigation and resolutions protecting human rights.[60] He eventually founded the Congo Reform Association, which worked to lobby the great powers into reforming the Congo through horrific photos collected by missionaries, public seminars, mass rallies, celebrity endorsements, and continuous press.[61]

His greatest weapon was knowledge. In addition to his own firsthand accounts, he was able to convince missionaries and others working in the Congo to expose the practices they saw. By 1908, Morel's movement had created enough pressure that the Congo was annexed to Belgium, where it would be subject to more rules and scrutiny than its current place in the "secretive royal fief," as Morel described it.[62]

---

56   Ibid.
57   Ibid.
58   Ibid.
59   Ibid.
60   Ibid.
61   Ibid.
62   Ibid.

Morel was an individual with very few resources or connections who worked hard to expose the complex inter-workings of a system controlled or backed by the most powerful countries on the planet. He had powerful enemies, most notably King Leopold of Belgium, but no matter how much he lost, he knew he needed to be the voice for others who couldn't speak or whose point of view were seen as less significant. His message had won the hearts of citizens, authors, and even big organizations like the Church of England and American religious groups. He turned an unknown system of terror into a worldwide cause for outrage and action. It would be inaccurate to say he stopped all the atrocities that occurred in King Leopold's Congo, but he created the mold many activists to this day follow. More importantly, he shows us that a relatively poor man raised by a single mother can galvanize the world with his passion.

* * *

One of the main things people underestimate is how much individuals matter. Yes, those responsible for most of the polluting need to be held accountable, but their power doesn't diminish yours. The reason we keep struggling to accept this so much is because we don't believe in our own power and the seeming impossibility that your individual decision not to take a plastic bag from the grocery store is going to stop climate change. We constantly teeter between viewing ourselves as small and feeling restless to do something. This is because we aren't looking at individual action the right way. We assume all our actions happen in a vacuum and humans aren't social creatures who interact with one another.

"I say to you today, my friends, that in spite of the difficulties and frustrations of the moment, I still have a dream."

In August 1963, Martin Luther King, Jr. stood in front of the Lincoln Memorial and told 250,000 people he had a dream for the future.[63] He poignantly stated African Americans have been enslaved, discriminated against, and deprived of the American promises of freedom. Rather than giving in, King painted a picture of a better America and because of his vision, we no longer live in the same society of his time.

He told the crowd, "We cannot walk alone. And as we walk, we must make the pledge that we shall march ahead. We cannot turn back."[64]

By 1964, King's movement led to the ratification of the 24th Amendment, which abolished poll taxes that restricted African Americans from voting, and the Civil Rights Act of 1964, which outlawed racial segregation in public facilities, education, and employment.[65]

Individual people matter in the way they use their voice and actions to create change. Studies have shown social norms are more influential than financial incentives in changing behavior toward the environment.[66]

---

63 History.com Editors, "'I Have a Dream' Speech," *History*, January 15, 2020.

64 Ibid.

65 History.com Editors, "Martin Luther King, Jr. born," *History*, January 15, 2020,

66 Susan Koger, Kerry E. Leslie, and Erica D. Hayes, "Climate Change: Psychological Solutions and Strategies for Change," *ResearchGate*, December 2011.

If individual people don't matter, why do we have streets named after them? Why do we have national holidays to celebrate one person—holidays deemed so important public institutions close and kids don't have to go to school? It is because holidays like Martin Luther King, Jr. Day don't just celebrate one person; they celebrate a legacy of action and change.

* * *

It is the people who become symbols of something larger, galvanizing support and commitment to a cause, who create the most change. Mohammad Bouazizi was a street vendor in Tunisia who dreamed of owning a pick-up truck.[67] Seemingly, this was a man who was powerless to the actions of the Tunisian dictator Zine El Abidine Ben Ali.[68] After years of police officials stealing his products, harassing him about vendor licenses, and humiliating him publicly, Bouazizi became desperate.

Bouazizi stood in the middle of traffic and yelled, "How do you expect me to make a living?" before lighting himself on fire.[69]

That day, he lit a spark that resonated with those who had been oppressed in Tunisia. It wasn't long before protests and violence broke out across the country. Within a month, Sine El Abidine Ben Ali, the president of Tunisia, fled the country and Tunisia eventually democratized. Bouazizi's singular

---

67 Caitlin O'Connell, "15 Ordinary People Who Changed History," *Reader's Digest*, Accessed May 3, 2020.

68 Ibid.

69 Bob Simon, "How a slap sparked Tunisia's revolution," *CBS News*, February 22, 2011.

action sparked protests and uprisings throughout the region and led to the Arab Spring movement.[70] Collective suffering transformed into collective action because of one man.

The Tiananmen Tank Man is an infamous photo depicting a single man standing in the way of four tanks in order to stop the Chinese military from forcefully suppressing the student-led demonstrations in Tiananmen Square. Although they were never able to identify him, he is a symbol of resistance to oppression. Ironically, the man without a name has been remembered for decades and has inspired other protests around the world.

All Rosa Parks did was refuse to give up her seat in the white section of a city bus and move to the back and yet we recognize her defiance and bravery as a turning point in the Civil Rights Movement.[71] Her single action sparked the Montgomery Bus Boycott, which began the day after Parks' arrest and lasted until the Supreme Court ruled segregated buses as unconstitutional almost a year later.

"There were times when it would have been easy to fall apart or to go in the opposite direction, but somehow I felt that if I took one more step, someone would come along to join me,"[72] *Parks said.*

Individual actions matter because they allow others to join in the fight and bring attention to the big issues many ignore or

---

70 Ibid.
71 Ibid.
72 Biography.com Editors, "Rosa Parks Biography," *Biography*, April 24, 2020.

tolerate. Individuals are responsible for creating social norms. As with most things, the law reflects attitudes, which is why people matter so much. It is much easier to succeed when people share your viewpoint than when you are constantly fighting against the tide.

These stories show all it takes is one person's determination to cause historic change. Beyond iconic names—like Rosa Parks and Martin Luther King, Jr.—are equally important people who have drastically change the world.

In March of 1980, Candy Lightner's daughter was killed by a drunk driver who had multiple DWIs.[73] At the time, few legal consequences for drunk driving and less negative views toward the issue existed.[74] She founded Mothers Against Drunk Driving (MADD) and fought until there were stricter laws across the United States. Since its inception, MADD has reportedly helped reduce drunk driving deaths by 50 percent, saving approximately 350,000 lives.[75] Today, driving while under the influence of alcohol or drugs is strictly punished but, more importantly, it is widely and emphatically untolerated by the general public.

The biggest difference between influential people with high name recognition and everyone else is that the former have had their stories elevated through their celebrity. My goal in writing this book is to expose the important work changemakers around the world do. As important as the

---

73 Editorial Staff, "Effectiveness of Mothers Against Drunk Driving," Alcohol.org, March 30, 2020.
74 Ibid.
75 Ibid.

contributions these icons have made are, millions of amazing people are not being recognized. The point is not solely to praise those making a difference but to remind everyone other people care and are willing to take action as a result. A large barrier to collective action is the shared belief that you alone care about the issue, which is just not true.

I know individual changemakers matter because I know how much certain people have impacted my life—not just in the way they make me a better person but in the way they make the world a better place. My grandma, Geraldine Fox, used to teach preschool before she caught mumps from a pupil and became deaf in one ear. Initially, she did not wear a hearing aid like many other young people with her condition and continued living her life without telling most people about her impairment. When she learned about the Deafness Research Foundation, Fox insisted they were not making enough money to cure deafness and set out to raise money. Fox had five kids at the time but started traveling to Washington, DC, and going door-to-door in Congress. She was so persistent she eventually convinced members of Congress to establish the National Institute on Deafness and Other Communication Disorders. In an interview with the foundation, she stated, "If you're passionate about curing something for a loved one or for yourself, then you've got to get involved. You can't just wait for somebody else to do it."[76]

Not only do people help create social norms, but we are also highly influenced by what those around us do. In the

---

76 National Institute on Deafness and other Communication Disorders Staff, "Podcast Interview with Geraldine Dietz Fox, Patient Advocate," National Institute on Deafness and other Communication Disorders, July 11, 2019.

now-famous Asch conformity experiment, a subject would routinely answer a simple multiple-choice question wrong 37 percent of the time and 75 percent gave a wrong answer at least once.[77] This wasn't because they didn't know the answer, but because the other people in the room with them were actors who would unanimously give an incorrect answer.[78] If just one actor gave the correct answer, only 5 percent of subjects still gave the wrong answer.[79] Another study tested the Asch conformity experiment by watching what individuals do when all the other people in an elevator are facing a certain direction.[80] Time and time again, the subject turned to face the same direction as the others, even if there was no door there. Subjects even continued to move and face different walls during the ride to match the other participants.[81] Although these are just small experiments, they demonstrate the extent to which people take their cues from those around them.

The world we live in and our willingness to speak up or act is directly connected to those around us. So, if just one person takes action, more people will quickly follow suit.

It seems counterintuitive but individual people matter because of what they can do collectively. While your decision not to waste an extra plastic bag doesn't make much of a dent

77 Saul McLeod, "Solomon Asch—Conformity Experiment," *Simple Psychology*, December 28, 2018.

78 Ibid.

79 Ibid.

80 Maria Popova, "Elevator Groupthink: An Ingenious 1962 Psychology Experiment in Conformity," *Brain Pickings*, Accessed May 4, 2020.

81 Ibid.

in global waste, when a larger group of individuals believe it matters to bring reusable bags to the grocery store instead of using plastic bags, they trigger others to do the same. This collective decision makes a small dent in the number of plastic bags used and shows producers there is less demand for them. Again, we don't exist in a vacuum.

Shannon Watts was a stay-at-home mom with seventy-five Facebook friends and an active Twitter account when she watched the Sandy Hook Elementary school shooting on TV and decided she was done ignoring the endless stream of mass shootings.[82] She created a Facebook page and, in a month, thousands rallied with her in Washington demanding action from politicians.[83] Her organization, Moms Demand Action, now has more members than the National Rifle Association.[84] She attributes finding her voice to the fierceness that comes with being a mother, and it is that passion that drove her to build a movement.

Watts told NBC's Know Your Value, "I bet on that being the emotion that would win the day. The NRA had made gun extremists afraid that their guns would be taken away, but I bet that eighty million moms in this country, regardless of political party, were afraid that their children would be taken away."[85]

---

82 Ginny Brzezinski, "How Shannon Watts went from stay-at-home mom to founder of the largest gun violence prevention org in the U.S.," *NBC News*, March 4, 2020.

83 Ibid.

84 Ibid.

85 Ibid.

Not only has she made a difference, but her actions have also inspired others to join the cause and even some to run for office. Lucy McBath, who lost her seventeen-year old son to gun violence in 2012, became an advocate and national spokesperson for Mom's Demand Action.[86] She has continued advocating gun violence prevention laws after winning Georgia's sixth congressional district.[87]

* * *

Lathika Chandra Mouli would never have started Evergo, which creates economic incentives for people to invest in solar energy and diversifies the energy mix cities rely on, if it was not for the influence of other people. Mouli originally conceived of her technology as a product for new markets. It was not until the United Nations recognized the potential her technology had to help the climate that she changed her approach. At the United Nations' education modules and startup program, Mouli worked with other innovators to further develop their technology and create something larger than themselves. Since leaving the program, she has joined different non-governmental organizations (NGOs), volunteered for nonprofits focusing on sustainability, educated the masses on the impact of daily decisions on the environment, and started many more projects focused on tackling climate change. The individuals she met at the United Nations Environment Asia Pacific Low Carbon Lifestyles Challenge influenced her life and her technology will influence many more.

---

86 Ibid.
87 Ibid.

According to extensive research on 323 campaigns from 1900 to 2006, political scientist Erica Chenoweth found it only takes 3.5 percent of a population engaged in active and sustained nonviolent campaigns to force political change.[88] This still comes out to about eleven million people in the United States, but given 66 percent of Americans are worried about climate change, all we need is a little action.[89] Even on a smaller scale, if 3.5 percent of your community demand change, you will succeed and the effects can ripple outward.

Very little demonstrates the rapid change in the rules of a society more than the #MeToo movement. Harvey Weinstein's sexual abuse of women was known as one of Hollywood's open secrets and yet it wasn't until a few brave women came forward that the world began to consider and address this persistent problem. If everyone in Hollywood knew, why didn't anything change before?

Sometimes, in situations like this, social norms can be harmful. I'm sure there were many individual motivations or reasons to ignore the issue of sexual abuse, most notably the belief that no one would take the allegations seriously. But much of it boils down to the bystander effect.[90] This facet of social psychology claims individuals are less likely to help a victim when there are other people present.[91] As

---

88   TEDx, "The success of nonviolent civil resistance: Erica Chenoweth at TEDxBoulder," November 4, 2013, Video, 12:33.

89   Ibid.

90   Psychology Today Staff, "Bystander Effect," *Psychology Today*, Accessed May 4, 2020.

91   Ibid.

it turns out, the need to conform socially causes us to do things that don't make a lot of sense. This can be seen in the case of Kitty Genovese, when witnesses watched a man brutally attack and kill a woman on the street and stared rather than stepped in.[92] Thirty-eight people watched this atrocity without raising their voices.[93] This is an extreme example but it demonstrates the effect people have on each other. The more people around you, the more likely it is you believe someone else will do something and the less it seems like your duty to step in. Just one person stepping up matters.

> *Robert F. Kennedy once said, "Each time a man stands up for an ideal, or acts to improve the lot of others, or strikes out against injustice, he sends forth a tiny ripple of hope, and crossing each other from a million different centers of energy and daring, those ripples build a current that can sweep down the mightiest walls of oppression and resistance."*

The world would certainly not be the same if it was not for the incredible actions of individuals like Candy Lightner, E.D. Morel, and Shannon Watts—most of whom you probably have never heard of. Without you even knowing about them, these individuals have made you safer and created a more prosperous future. Imagine what the world would look like if we all acknowledged our capacity for change.

---

92 Ibid.
93 Ibid.

JUST REMEMBER:

1. There are people everywhere, beyond those we easily recognize, who are making a difference. Why not join them?

2. You don't need lots of resources or connections to change the world.

3. Individuals matter because of the way they influence others.

CHAPTER 4

MILLIONS OF SMALL LEAPS

―――

THE IMPORTANCE OF TAKING RISKS

I always wondered why somebody didn't do something about that. Then I realized I AM SOMEBODY.

—LILY TOMLIN

Ben Cohen and Jerry Greenfield are not your typical businessmen. Jerry had been rejected from multiple medical schools and Ben had gone to five universities before dropping out and deciding to teach pottery to special needs kids in the Adirondacks.[94] They were both looking for something to do and decided to start a bagel store. After learning how expensive the equipment was, they settled on ice cream and moved to Burlington, VT.[95]

―――

94 Guy Raz, "Ben & Jerry's: Ben Cohen And Jerry Greenfield (2017)," March 22, 2020, *How I Built This,* From *NPR,* Podcast audio, Accessed April 26, 2020.

95 Ibid.

Neither of them had ever started a business or seemed to have any of the necessary skills. Vermont is known for its brutal winters and Ben had a poor sense of smell and taste, making ice cream a strange choice.[96] Nevertheless, Ben and Jerry's Ice Cream was born and is now one of the biggest ice cream brands in the world. Jerry describes the experience as "falling down on the side of a cliff trying to grab onto whatever branch was there you can hold onto."[97] There was no plan—just passion and the drive to push themselves off the cliff.

Ben and Jerry were not prepared to be CEOs. In fact, when the business began to take off, they tried to sell it because they didn't see themselves as business owners and did not even believe in big businesses to begin with.[98] It wasn't until a friend encouraged them to try designing a more ethical business that the duo decided to remain involved in the company.[99] But their unique ideas and unconventional style is what made Ben and Jerry's a success as well as a progressive company. Most companies avoid politics, but Ben and Jerry had no interest in just selling ice cream. Their company has come out in support of Black Lives Matter, Occupy Wall Street, LBGT equality, environmental justice, and many other issues.[100] Their starting salary is twice the minimum wage, their brownies are made by a bakery dedicated to employing previously incarcerated people, and community service is part of their mission statement.[101]

---

96 Ibid.
97 Ibid.
98 Ibid.
99 Ibid.
100 Ben and Jerry's Staff, "Issues We Care About," Ben and Jerry's, Accessed May 4, 2020.
101 Catherine Taibi, "9 Reasons To Love Ben & Jerry's That Have Nothing To Do With Ice Cream," *HuffPost*, August 15, 2013.

Now imagine a world in which Jerry decided to become a cross-country truck driver and Ben continued pursuing his career in pottery as they both had planned. The decision to spend their last dollars on an abandoned gas station that would become their first store was a leap of faith and the world is better for it.

No one ever has it all figured out but we will need more people taking leaps into the unknown if we are going to tackle the climate crisis.

* * *

People often believe someone else will find the silver bullet and the weight of the issue will no longer bear so heavily on them.[102] Diffusion of responsibility is a coping mechanism that allows people to ignore their own inaction.[103] This denial is counterproductive. If everyone believes someone else will handle it, no one will. Since no individual can take on climate change as a whole, it is the responsibility of the group to take action. Yet, rather than working together we assume someone else will step up.

In 2013, the World Health Organization announced that Delhi, India, was the most polluted city in the world. For the citizens, it was not hard to see the problem. The chief

---

102 Daniel R. Abbasi, "Americans and Climate Change: Closing the Gap Between Science and Action," Yale School of Forestry and Environmental Studies, 2005.

103 Ibid.

minister went as far as to call it a "gas chamber."[104] Ever since Amit Singh learned about the damage to Delhi's air quality, he began looking for a solution. Just like that, he saw it as his problem to solve. There was no wavering, no blaming others, no questioning his place. Singh's company Parimukh Innovations Pvt purifies air as a vehicle moves without consuming any power. The government of India is currently piloting the project with great results. The biodegradable filters have been installed in thirty buses and collected 1.5 kilograms of dust in just ten days. They have also created filters for rickshaws and motorcycles.[105] No matter what obstacle he came across, Singh kept pushing forward for the same reason he started.

"When you see patients coughing like hell in front of you, you always see what you can do from your side [to help]. And that is why from my capability of environmental technology, I kept on working on this idea."

In fact, most of the people I interviewed behaved this way. They were either disappointed with the situation and response from leaders or found a way to help and charged forward.

As people around the world celebrated the latest attempt at global collective action, the Paris Climate Accord, innovators like Hugh Weldon and Ahmad Mu'azzam were only becoming more frustrated with the lack of tangible changes. Initially, they were delighted the world had come together to create this agreement but the more they thought about it, the angrier they became. They realized that although some of the most

---

104 Umair Irfan, "How Delhi became the most polluted city on earth," *Vox Media*, November 25, 2017.

105 Evocco Staff, "About," Accessed May 24, 2020.

powerful people in the world were talking about the issue, very little was actually going to come of their high-level discussions. Hugh and Ahmad could not sit idly by and watch the world's leaders talk about change for the sake of talking.

Food production accounts for 26 percent of global greenhouse gas emissions and is a decision most people make three times a day.[106] Hugh and Ahmad decided this was a great place to try and change behaviors. The pair refined their idea by constantly getting feedback until they eventually created Evocco, an app that scores the sustainability of grocery receipts, tracks your progress, and shows you the best food options based on nutrition and climate impact. If individuals were going to make a difference, they would need to be informed. Evocco's model works by providing real-time feedback and actionable steps that encourage people to improve over time. It is a brilliant idea that allows consumers to not only make changes to their lives but also eat healthier as well. With this aggregated knowledge of their food's impact, there is more possibility for consumer-led changes to industry.

Hugh and Ahmad were unwilling to wait for governments to take real initiative on the problem and instead took huge leaps in their own lives.

In the early days, led by visions of change and fueled by passion, the duo made big sacrifices like moving back home with their parents and taking part time jobs. "We are trying to compensate for limited resources and experience with enthusiasm and passion.... Bar a few grey hairs on Hugh's head

---

106 Parimukh Staff, "About Us," Parimukh, Accessed March 22, 2020.

and my incapability of staying awake through a full movie, we have thoroughly enjoyed the experience so far," Ahmad told Silicon Republic.[107]

It was not just their initial bold decisions that allowed them to progress but millions of small leaps of faith along the way. Like most startups, they began running into cash flow issues and at one point had to rebuild the product after deciding it wasn't done correctly. Rather than give in, they came back to the same question with every obstacle they faced: "Do you feel that you played every card here and how much [do] you believe in the mission?"

Hugh and Ahmad were unwilling to give up until they felt they had exhausted all their options but, more than that, their belief in the mission propelled them forward in their darkest moments. A lack of resources did not stop them from starting Evocco and their passion pushed them past obstacles to take risks.

* * *

Alhaji Siraj Bah founded Rusgal Trading as a homeless teen in Sierra Leone after a devastating mudslide killed his friends and family. He did not wait for anyone to save him. Rather, he decided to use whatever he could to begin solving this issue plaguing his entire country.

But what was it about Bah that made him feel this responsibility?

---

107 John Kennedy, "Evocco teaches consumers how to be sustainable shoppers," *Silicon Republic*, November 12, 2018.

At the time, he only had twenty dollars so it wasn't a particularly stable or wise financial decision. Most people would have decided there were other people in a better place to attempt this feat, but he didn't wait. He didn't possess any seemingly superior intellectual ability given he had dropped out of school at age thirteen and hadn't been trained in this field. The only difference seemed to be his motivation. Like the Nike slogan, he "just did it."

"You must never wait for the right time because the time is always right. With whatsoever little you have in your possession, use it, be innovative and creative, be a changemaker, believe in yourself, and be hardworking."

He had nothing except the internal need and desire to make changes.

In fact, according to a survey conducted by Bashaw and Grant in 1994, motivation is a more significant factor in overall career success than intelligence, ability, and salary.[108]

Declarations of change mean nothing if you don't take action. Picture the Rocky montage. Beyond the inspirational music, it depicts Rocky sweating, punching, and running until he reaches the top of the famed Rocky Steps at the Philadelphia Museum of Art. That's where all montages start—at the moment the protagonist decides to commit to something

---

108 Edward Bashaw and Stephen Grant, "Exploring the Distinctive Nature of Work Commitments: Their Relationships with Personal Characteristics, Job Performance, and Propensity to Leave," *Journal of Personal Selling and Sales Management*, October 2013.

bigger than themselves. Rather than giving in to fear, the protagonist begins their training.

As it turns out, avoiding things that scare you only leads to feelings of failure.[109] The only way to overcome it is exposure.[110]

In 1986, at a symposium on "Future Style," famed author Ray Bradbury told those listening to "jump off the cliff and learn how to make wings on the way down."[111] This lack of a plan runs contrary to most things we are told but it's sometimes necessary to stop overthinking.

Over the years, this idea has been consistently repeated. Airline executive Franco Mancassola told the *Sunday Times* of London that he lives by the rule, "Jump out of the plane and build your wings on the way."[112]

Reid Hoffman, recent co-founder of LinkedIn, said, "Entrepreneurship is jumping off a cliff and assembling a plane on the way down."[113]

It sounds inspirational in a tweet but assembling a plane is no easy task, especially as you metaphorically plummet toward the ground. But when Bradbury was later asked if he had ever

---

109 Noam Shpancer, "Overcoming Fear: The Only Way Out is Through," *Psychology Today*, September 20, 2020,

110 Ibid.

111 Quote Investigator Staff, "Jump Off the Cliff and Build Your Wings on the Way Down," *Quote Investigator*, October 30, 2015.

112 Ibid.

113 Ibid.

failed to build his wings in time, he replied, "All of my life, I've jumped off the cliff and built my wings. It works every single time. It never fails."[114]

This magic engineerial feat also highlights a certain level of fearlessness that Bah seemed to display. Remember, he was living on the streets with no safety net or money, a condition we traditionally consider disadvantaged. But in the spirit of being optimistic, we can begin to imagine how, at this low point, the fear of failure dissipates and you are left with nowhere to go but up. I'm not suggesting this level of tragedy is necessary for action but it's important to remember that no one is prevented from taking action because of their situation.

Our lives would be significantly different if we did not take risks.

When my mom graduated college in California, she knew she wanted to be in Asia. That's about all she knew. She had spent time backpacking around the area and heard it was easy to get a job in Hong Kong, so she packed a single bag and bought a one-way ticket.

She had never been to Hong Kong before landing with one night booked at a hotel and no job. It was Chinese New Year, meaning all the stores were closed. But that had not even crossed her mind until she landed. It was a huge leap of faith. She knew no one there and did not have the tiniest inkling of a plan. It was there that she met my dad.

---

114 Ibid.

My mom describes it as the scariest thing she ever did but staying in the US and getting a desk job was her worst nightmare, so she took a one-way flight to an unknown life. People take risks every day and without my mom's brave decision, I would not exist.

Turns out jumping off a cliff and learning to fly takes very little resources—just the motivation and dedication to blindly throw yourself into the unknown. If a pottery teacher and a med school reject can create a six-billion-dollar ice cream company, anyone can take a risk.

JUST REMEMBER:
1. Stop waiting for other people to solve problems for you.

2. Motivation is more important than fear and lack of resources. Figure out what you care about the most, and take the leap.

3. Spend less time worried about the outcome and more time focused on the impact you want to have.

CHAPTER 5

ARE YOU GUYS MAKING BOMBS IN THERE?

———

NO ONE SETS OUT TO CHANGE THE WORLD

We can't claim our ink will solve the world's pollution problem, but it does show what can be done if you look at this problem slightly differently.

—ANIRUDH SHARMA

As I began looking around the world for innovators to talk to, I became increasingly inspired by their drive and determination. But in trying to demystify these qualities, I had forgotten they exist everywhere.

Jack is a sixteen-year-old who grew up in a small town in Colorado. He can be found wearing the same Eagles sweater depicting the final score of the February 4, 2018 Eagles–Patriots game (PHL: 41, NE: 33) and floppy Nike shoes held together with so much neon green/orange duct-tape that Michael Jordan wouldn't recognize them. The only discernible difference in his day-to-day appearance is his pants, which alternate between sweatpants and basketball shorts, depending on the season.

After gaining some environmental consciousness in middle school, he set out to build solar panels to be placed at and used by his middle school. He began applying for local and state grants to fund the roughly half-a-million-dollar panels and convinced the school to undertake the project. He scoured the valley for grants and, so far, has raised $250,000. He has been working with a local solar implementation entrepreneur to add legitimacy and experience to the project. Jack faced a lot of pushback with his initial plan to sell the roof of the school and have the administration buy energy credits with an option to buy the roof back in five years. Instead, he is now raising the $500,000 through grants and donations. He also struggled to be taken seriously and would often have teachers send emails out for him because adults seemed to respond better to other adults. Through his persistence, he eventually proved he was serious about the project.

Maybe it's because Jack is my younger brother and I'll always dismiss him as a real person or maybe it's because I didn't even know he had done all of this until a combination of old teachers, family friends, and local city council members filled in the story of my incredible brother. I just never thought of him as a young innovator. As much as I've loved my 3 a.m. calls to India or Sierra Leone, I could have just called home. There are amazing people all around us, who no UN Environmental or Peace Award would recognize but are just as important. Human beings everywhere are amazing.

I recently called my mom to tell her about my day and was met with chaos on the other end.

"Jack, I swear if you fall off the roof, I'm going to be pissed off!"

I had clearly interrupted a more important conversation. When I naturally asked what my brother was doing on the roof, she told me he had figured out how to buy small solar panels online and was trying to set them up on our roof. The innovation never stops and neither does he.

His room now looks like a hospital ward as he has replaced all the lights with LED lights powered by a hundred-watt solar array, leaving an eerie, bright glow that streams into the hallway. The switch for the lights in his room has been duct taped down to stop anyone from accidentally turning them on. The solar panels offset all his energy needs from heating and lights to his computer and phone. He has also stopped eating red meat and set up a composting station in our house. He specified some of these personal steps won't solve the overall problem but while we push for legislative change, he feels responsible for making changes to avoid feeling like a hypocrite. It can be hard to make changes to your life when you feel like you're the only one sacrificing for it but Jack states that this is necessary. Jack believes you have to hold yourself to certain standards so others know how to take action.

"I think it's impossible to go completely net zero. It just is because our lives are so dependent on it, but you have to set a precedent for yourself and others while these other changes are taking place."

We are constantly told to "dream big and reach for the moon so we may land among the stars," but what if that's the wrong attitude? While in some cases thinking big inspires big actions, in the case of climate change, it seems to mostly inspire fear. It's not good logic for astronauts and it's not great for combatting these large-scale issues from an individual perspective either.

Right now, we are presented with one huge task: solve climate change. But like any problem, it needs to be broken down into manageable pieces. This is a mental leap we still haven't been able to make because we are trying to do it on our own. As each of us begin to break down the monster that is climate change, you find a plethora of equally scary monsters. As a macro issue, climate change can be simplified as just too much carbon or fossil fuel use. But when you begin examining it more critically, you realize it is a collection of issues like deforestation, over-consumption, and air pollution, all of which require unique solutions. While this means there is no one solution that fixes it all, it also means people can take a variety of approaches.

In fact, the more I began talking to people around the world, the more I realized no one sets out to solve overall climate change. Each innovator simply saw a local problem affecting them and found a creative solution. This is easily demonstrated in how connected their innovations are to their immediate surroundings.

Amit Singh, Arpit Dhupar, and Anirudh Sharma, all from India, have focused on combating pollution and turning it into other products, such as ink. Isabella O'Brien from Canada conducted research on ocean acidification after realizing it was ruining the lake where she spent her summers. Amber Sparks and Emily Hazelwood of Blue Latitudes, a company turning oil platforms into reefs, both grew up near the sea. They also met at college in San Diego, and Emily's first job out of college was working as a field technician on the British Petroleum oil spill of 2010 in the Gulf of Mexico. Cecil and Alhaji created charcoal alternatives out of carbonized agricultural waste and coconut husks to power their communities after a damaging landslide and a coal ban.

While it seems obvious you would be inspired to fix the things affecting you the most, it just proves you don't need to go far to search for problems or solutions. All these eco-innovators are deeply passionate about the earth. But when I asked about what convinced them to start their companies, not one of them began with their need to take on climate change in its entirety. They all wanted to tell me about their communities, how they had noticed a problem, and what they did to fix it.

On a trip back to India while he was in college, Anirudh Sharma took a photo of the exhaust coming from a diesel generator.[115] Streaming out of the generator, what Sharma described as a sign of human progress, was a triangular cloud of black exhaust.[116] The photo fascinated him as he recognized how deadly the industrialization process had been on

---

115   TED, "Ink made of air pollution | Anirudh Sharma," February 8, 2013, Video, 8:24.

116   Ibid.

the health of people in his home country. Returning to MIT, he began experimenting by burning candles and mixing it with vegetable oil and vodka.[117] It wasn't anything fancy but he was able to create a rudimentary version of ink that could be fed into a cartridge.[118] Two years after seeing the initial photo, he moved back to India to set up a lab and founded AIR-INK.[119] His early prototypes of a device that would capture emissions attached to diesel cars looked like something out of a Dr. Seuss book and would often catch on fire.[120] This created quite a sight, causing skepticism and thoughts like, *"What are these guys doing? Are they making bombs in there?"*[121]

AIR-INK eventually created a device that would collect pollution from static stations like diesel generators and could capture 95 percent of the pollution produced.[122] The ink could be made into pens holding forty to fifty minutes of car pollution.[123] Skeptics were quick to tell him turning pollution into ink wasn't a real business—it was just something fun.

The first people to embrace his product were artists. Because every pollution source is different, the ink produced created a slightly different black color each time and was quickly picked up by artists around the world.[124] His company became so well-known polluters from around the world started sending

---

117 Ibid.
118 Ibid.
119 Ibid.
120 Ibid.
121 Ibid.
122 Ibid.
123 Ibid.
124 Ibid.

him bags of pollution in the hopes he could create something useful from it rather than paying waste management companies to dispose of it or dumping it into rivers.[125] Despite the wide-reaching impact of his company, he has—on multiple occasions—told people his invention isn't a "silver bullet" but a reminder that people everywhere can turn waste into something useful. Sharma believes his product is not just an ink but a messaging tool. He envisions a world in which cities print their newspapers with ink made of their own pollution.

"Imagine a million people waking up to that newspaper. The amount of awareness that raises they would probably wouldn't drive their car to work. They would probably take public transport. All that is a bigger building of a movement around this problem right now. That is really powerful to us."[126]

His ink became a tool to spread awareness through sustainable art, but he didn't set out to inspire artists or exterminate all the pollution in the world. He was simply inspired by a photo of stark black pollution coming from a diesel generator and decided he could turn something affecting the health of people in his country into something more useful.

* * *

Focusing on the whole world is actually dangerous, in this case, as it leads to more hopelessness and less action. Psychologists at the University of Pennsylvania, Carnegie Mellon University, and Decision Research conducted an experiment

---

125 Ibid.
126 Nick Yulman and Zakiya Gibbons, February 20, 2019, "Unnatural Resources," Podcast audio, *Just The Beginning,* Accessed December 22, 2019.

in which researchers showed one group a picture and description of a little girl who needed food aid and the other group the same photo and statistical information detailing the millions of starving people who needed aid.[127] Because people in the second group felt they could make less of an impact, they donated less.[128] This phenomenon of people being less willing to help an individual when they learn about the full extent of the problem is called pseudoinefficacy.[129]

As with many global issues, we cannot examine the whole problem at once with hopes of discerning solutions. We simply are not programmed to handle problems this big and trying to examine them through a global lens only makes us less active in solving them. Humans are also notoriously bad at understanding problems as they become bigger. Again, psychologists have come up with a convenient name for our mental shortcoming: Psychic numbing stipulates that as the number of people suffering increases, our sympathy declines.[130] This is yet another reason why individuals need to use a local lens and focus on immediate surroundings.

So maybe for a second we stop dreaming big and start thinking about the individual lives we can change. In Jennifer Beckner's TED Talk, she discussed the power of individuals.[131]

---

127 Deborah Small, George Loewenstein, and Paul Slovic, "Sympathy and callousness: The impact of deliberative thought on donations to identifiable and statistical victims," *Science Direct*, July 7, 2005.

128 Ibid.

129 Ibid.

130 Paul Slovic, "Psychic Numbing and Genocide," *American Psychological Association*, November 2007.

131 TEDx, "The power of the individual | Jennifer Beckner | TEDxMSU," April 15, 2016, Video, 7:52.

Throughout college, she volunteered for the Lansing Refugee Development Center, which helps over 1,700 newcomers in Lansing with social and academic support.[132] It was easy to be overwhelmed by the 60 million displaced people around the world but she was able to find the impact in helping just one.[133]

Beckner told the crowd, "We are intimidated by the fact that we can't be Mother Teressa or Nelson Mandela, so we think we can't do anything. But even Mother Teresa said that the solution is not to do great things but small things with great love."[134]

In our globalized society, we are more aware of what is going on around the world than ever before but our brains can only handle so much input. As a tradeoff, we see most issues as global rather than stemming from a combination of individual and local problems we have direct connections and access to.

Beckner finished her talk by stating, "Focusing at this macro level can lead to an awareness without investment. We will throw our concern at an issue from far away, but we see it as a number, not as something personal. When you truly invest in an individual involved, you're able to see people as people."[135]

Instead of fixating on the scope of the refugee problem, she focuses on the individuals she can help at the Lansing Refugee Development Center where she makes a tangible difference.

---

132 Ibid.
133 Ibid.
134 Ibid.
135 Ibid.

* * *

Those who set out to change the world quickly realize it can't be done in one fell swoop. The only way to do it is to focus on individual people and problems.

Samantha Powers grew up reading books in the basement of an Irish pub while her father drank upstairs.[136] When she was nine years old, Powers immigrated to the United States.[137] In the 1990s, she began seeing images of emaciated people and death camps in Bosnia.[138] After being denied from every non-governmental organization (NGO) in Washington, DC, that helped Bosnian refugees, she became a war correspondent covering the Yugoslav Wars at twenty-three years old.[139] These photos had compelled her to go to the Balkans, despite admittedly having no skills or capacity to act on how to best solve this travesty.[140] There, she was able to elevate the stories of people struggling and pressure the United States government to take action.[141]

She wrote *A Problem from Hell: America and the Age of Genocide*, a book that brings attention to the terrors of genocide around the world. She went on to win a Pulitzer Prize for her work.[142]

---

136 Samantha Power, The Education of an Idealist: *A Memoir,* New York City: Dey Street Books, 2019.

137 Ibid.

138 Ibid.

139 Ibid.

140 Ibid.

141 Ibid.

142 Moira Forbes, "Inside Samantha Power's Hard-Won Wisdom on Inspiring Action," *Forbes,* July 7, 2016.

Powers was then given a choice: to continue reporting in Bosnia in the hopes of persuading US policymakers to take action or go to Harvard Law School to hopefully change policy herself.[143] She chose Harvard and went on to work for Senator Barack Obama as a foreign policy fellow.[144] She never saw herself becoming part of the government she had criticized so strongly for her entire career, but she kept looking for ways to have more of an impact.[145]

In 2009, she was appointed to President Obama's National Security Council as a special assistant to the president and senior director for multilateral affairs and human rights, where she advocated for a military intervention in Libya on humanitarian grounds.[146]

In 2013, Powers became the twenty-eighth and youngest United States Ambassador to the United Nations.[147] Powers struggled to make as big of an impact as she would like but her work still changed lives.[148]

"People who care, act, and refuse to give up may not change the world, but they can change many individual worlds."[149]

For the twentieth anniversary of the 1995 World Conference on Women, China hosted a summit in tribute. However,

143 Ibid.
144 Ibid.
145 Ibid.
146 Samantha Power, The Education of an Idealist: A Memoir.
147 Ibid.
148 Ibid.
149 Ibid.

women in China and around the world were still being held as prisoners of war for speaking their mind.[150] Power started the #FreeThe20 campaign to highlight the stories of individual women on social media.[151] She posted pictures of each woman on the windows of the US Mission to the UN so everyone who walked by or into the building would be reminded of their plight.[152]

"In an atmosphere of repression and democratic backsliding around the world, I found it gratifying to focus less on the overall human rights 'recession'—an abstraction that could be paralyzing—and more on specific people. Once freed, these women would then be able to raise their voice on behalf of important causes."[153]

Within two years, Powers was able to get fourteen of the twenty women released. In highlighting these women's struggles, she was able to shed light on the issue around the world.[154] Despite this success, she lamented she wasn't able to do more. Even though she hadn't fixed the world's judicial system and treatment of women, she told the Mission's human rights advisor, "For each one of these women, and those around them, it is the universe."[155]

It all began with some photos showcasing atrocities occurring thousands of miles away and the need to do something.

---

150 Ibid.
151 Ibid.
152 Ibid.
153 Ibid.
154 Ibid.
155 Ibid.

For changemakers around the world, moments like these spark a lifetime of action. Samantha Powers is a changemaker not because she solved genocides, but because she made a choice to act, focusing on what she could accomplish.

"We decide, on issues large and small, whether we will be bystanders or upstanders."[156]

JUST REMEMBER:

1. No one sets out to change the world. Rather, they look to solve problems facing them and their communities.

2. It is impossible to solve the whole problem alone. Think about how climate change impacts you locally and focus on possible solutions for that problem.

3. Everyone has something to bring to the table. Think about how your skills are valuable in solving bigger issues.

---

156 Ibid.

CHAPTER 6

YES, BUT

EVEN GOOD IDEAS FACE RESISTANCE

"Hi, my name is Isabella, and I'm a grade ten student at West-mount Secondary School."[157]

Isabella O'Brien sits in front of a cabinet filled with figurines: a golden owl and a blue bunny statue. The lilac and blue walls of her room are reminiscent of a newborn's room that was never repainted. She is an unassuming character until she begins to use words like "dafnea pulex population." The video is titled, "Aquatic Osteoporosis - Remediating the emerging environmental problem of lake calcium decline," describing her experiments on ocean acidification.[158] It is in this moment you begin to understand how she was a 2015 Google science fair finalist at the age of thirteen. She is now a freshman at the University of Southern California hoping to shape environmental policy but has been making a difference since middle school.

---

157   Isabella O'Brien, "Aquatic Osteoporosis - Remediating the emerging environmental problem of lake calcium decline," March 22, 2017, Video, 3:54.

158   Ibid.

Growing up in Canada, she spent her summers at a lake. It didn't take much for her to notice the lake changed slightly every year she returned. Even to her young eye, she noticed fewer clams existed and the shells of crayfish were thinning and disappearing completely. Curious about what was going on, she set up a lab in her basement and began conducting experiments on the lake water. She didn't think much of the greater consequences of her work or what she could contribute to the world. She was just curious about her lake and what would fix the effects of the acidification she discovered. In fact, she conducted much of her research simply because her middle school was having a science fair. From there, she went on to compete in the national science fair, where she was exposed to other environmentally-minded students. It was there she saw firsthand the real-world impact students could have. Unburdened by the "adult" viewpoint, she continued with her work because at her age, there "doesn't seem to be any reason why you can't do it."

It wasn't until she was in ninth grade that she began experiencing the pushback of the "real-world" mindset. She had just finished presenting her project about using discarded seashells to combat ocean acidification in front of a room of technology visionaries and industry leaders who were acting as judges. Filled with nerves, she awaited feedback. Finally, one of the judges stood up and said, "You know, I just don't understand how this could work. It's just going to be too expensive." This was a science fair being judged by those who were supposed to be visionaries in their fields but they had immediately shut down the ideas of a passionate student. O'Brien stood there frustrated and discouraged. All she had done was propose an idea that could potentially solve a problem.

"I was in grade nine. I couldn't do a cost analysis of how much it was going to cost. It was an idea, right, and it's not like anybody else had an alternative idea."

In moments like these, it is so easy to give in and conform to the belief that you cannot make a difference because someone with more power said so. But that didn't stop O'Brien from dreaming. She had proven you could use something that is in excess—seashells—to fix a problem caused by human pollution—the acidification of our lakes. As the words of discouragement rang in her ears, she was able to find another professor who was awarded government grants to work on a similar project but used ash instead of shells. She was able to see there was a place for her world-changing research and people out there who could fund it. She ignored the critics and went to work with the professor.

Her story is proof that it just takes one person to show you progress is possible.

In any startup, there are countless failures. With eco-innovators, it is no different. But those who succeed have become masters at dealing with failure. When I first began interviewing innovators, I assumed coming up with the idea and creating it was the toughest part but I quickly learned that for most innovators, much of the struggle came after they had created or devised an alternative solution. As it turns out, even good ideas face resistance and often that makes them better. With every great idea comes hundreds of people insisting that if it was possible, it would have been done already. But it is with the courage of individuals who challenge the pushback that progress is made.

* * *

Offshore oil and gas platforms are a symbol of industry. They look extremely unnatural, jetting out of clear blue water in the middle of the ocean. Directly below the surface is a completely different world: a vibrant eco-system filled with so much wildlife that fishermen and divers alike flock to those locations. It is a testament to the strength of the environment, thriving in seemingly unnatural places.

It is this same dichotomy that piqued Emily Hazelwood's interest in these structures. It was while she was working as a field technician during the British Petroleum oil spill of 2010 in the Gulf of Mexico that Hazelwood first learned about the Rigs to Reefs program, whereby offshore oil and gas platforms are decommissioned as artificial reefs. However, it was not until she met Amber Sparks in graduate school and learned California also had a Rigs to Reefs program that the two friends began to think, "There are oil platforms in every ocean on the planet. Why aren't we doing this everywhere?"

Turning these oil platforms into reefs is not only good for the environment but can also result in millions of dollars in cost savings. Decommissioning oil and gas platforms as reefs, according to the Rigs to Reefs guidelines, saves approximately twenty-two million dollars per platform and creates opportunities for commercial and recreational fishing and scuba diving. Considering more than 6,000 oil and gas platforms exist worldwide, opportunities for action are abundant.

In 2015, the duo created Blue Latitudes, a marine environmental consulting firm, and began trying to figure out how to use this overlooked program to make their vision a reality.

Despite their many accomplishments, they have encountered setbacks just like every other startup. But their biggest lesson is that "success is really the ability to go from one failure to the next with a lot of enthusiasm."

Whenever they hit a seemingly insurmountable wall, they pivot and look for new opportunities and people who can help them. They also lean on each other to get through the hard moments because they both believe so strongly in the mission that failure is less difficult to deal with.

* * *

Daan Roosegaarde, a Dutch artist and innovator, summed up all the resistance he has ever received to his innovative ideas in two words: "Yes, but."[159] In his many years as a designer, he has created projects including a smog vacuum cleaner, "Waterlicht" ("a virtual reality combination of LEDs and lenses which create an ever changing virtual flood" that depicts what the world will look like if no one takes action on climate change), and the "Van Gogh Path" (a bike path that lights up and is powered by solar energy).[160]

159 TED, "A smog vacuum cleaner and other magical city designs | Daan Roosegaarde," September 19, 2017, Video, 12:18.
160 Daan Roosengaarde, "Projects" *Studio Roosegaarde*, Accessed January 4, 2019.

In his TED Talk, he states, "Let's not be afraid. Let's be curious."[161]

His creative projects all begin with a question. In the case of the smog vacuum cleaner, it was, "Why do we accept pollution?"[162] It was this question that changed the frightening Beijing smog he was living with at the time into inspiration.[163] He was able to create a vacuum that sucks up 30,000 cubic meters of air per hour, cleans the air on a nano level using little electricity, and releases it, creating areas that are 55–75 percent cleaner than the rest of the city.[164] But he wasn't done asking bold questions or making bold statements with his smog vacuum.[165] Next, he declared, "Waste should not exist."[166] He took the carbon the vacuum had collected and compressed it for thirty minutes to make diamond rings (1,000 cubic meters = 1 smog ring).[167] He had taken something that shortened people's lifespans and made them sick and turned it into a declaration of love.

Roosegaarde has noticed that as much as people say they want innovation in the abstract, he is continually met with variations of this phrase: "Yes, we love the idea, but it's too expensive or ugly. It's too difficult, it cannot be done."[168] The only reason the world has his innovations is because

---

161 TED, "A smog vacuum cleaner and other magical city designs | Daan Roosegaarde."
162 Ibid.
163 Ibid.
164 Ibid.
165 Ibid.
166 Ibid.
167 Ibid.
168 Ibid.

instead of listening to those people, he used their criticisms as an ingredient in his designs. He even went as far as to make a "yes, but" chair that administers a short but intense shock every time you say those two creatively destructive words.[169] Not only did this help his team recognize their negative thoughts, but it also drove away potential partners who wouldn't have fit in with the company vision.[170]

So this is step one: catching yourself when you fall into this trap. There is no need to embody the same mindset as the rest of the world. Plenty of people will try to tell you why your vision won't work—don't be one of them.

Arpit Dhupar is the founder of Chakr Innovations, a company that captures emissions from the exhaust of diesel generators without affecting the engine. Like many other innovators, Dhupar didn't think much about his decision to start a company, probably because it's hard to think when you can't breathe.

Dhupar was raised in Delhi, India, and when he was younger, he developed breathing problems. The doctors told him he could no longer play sports. It wasn't difficult to connect his health problems to the environment around him. Globally, over seven million premature deaths a year are linked to air pollution, and 1.2 million of those deaths occur in India alone.[171] In places like Delhi, it's more dangerous to exercise than not at all, rewriting even our basic assumptions about leading a healthy life.

---

169 Ibid.
170 Ibid.
171 Business Standard Staff, "Air pollution kills 1.2 mn Indians in a year, third biggest cause of death," *Business Standard*, April 3, 2019.

Despite being a mechanical engineer, Dhupar insists everyone is smart enough to solve these problems. But you may ask, if everyone is smart enough to do this, why are we in this situation at all?

It takes a certain amount of resilience and dedication to attack these problems.

Like a video game, every experience we've overcome moves us onto the next level. We have proven to ourselves that we can not only handle a tough situation, but we can also use those new skills to clear the next level. It's like in the Super Mario Bros video game—you can't defeat Bowser until you've jumped over all the mushrooms. Dhupar says believing in your abilities to overcome an issue, especially the big uncertain ones we all face, can help us conquer them.

"Whatever the situation be, no matter how tough, we, or the person who is in that situation [may be], [they are] the best person to tackle that situation. There is no one else who is better than you to solve the problem, for one simple reason: that our own past has trained us."

In the same way Mario needs to collect coins and defeat enough mushrooms to get to the next level in Super Mario Bros, no matter how many times he falls in a bottomless pit or is vanquished by a villain, he always starts again to save the princess. Yes, this is partially due to the fact that he is a computer program that will continually restart unless your gaming system crashes, but I like to believe it has something to do with his undying motivation to complete the mission, or as Dhupar calls it, "the problem statement." He believes every problem can be solved by identifying them as problem statements. Both have a goal they desperately want to acquire—Mario has Princess Peach and Dhupar has clean air.

During the beginning stages of Chakr Innovations, Dhupar and his team began to run into some mushrooms. They had not been able to pay their employees in two months and were not even able to reimburse them for the materials they had bought for the company. Around this time, they were working on a prototype to send to an important client when the product began leaking. With little time to fix the prototype before it had to be sent to the client, the unpaid team put in fourteen continuous hours of work as a last-ditch attempt. The weary-eyed, desperate group became increasingly frustrated as the hours ticked by and there was still no improvement. In those moments, the despair hung in the room, weighing down the group as moments of surrender flickered in their eyes. Exasperated, Dhupar turned to a colleague and asked him blankly, "Why is it that every time we have to do something, it is so difficult, and we are never able to meet our timeline? We are never able to fix it in the first try."

In those dark morning hours, his colleague responded, "You know why it is so difficult? Why every action we do is so difficult? Because the problem we are trying to solve is a very big problem."

There it was, the reminder that they were all there for a reason. Looking around the room, you could see a group of tired, unpaid people, and yet, they were all still there trying to fix the prototype. That moment stuck with him. Even when his employees were overworked or underpaid, they did not care about those immediate adversities because they believed in the better future their work would create. Dhupar began to see his employees motivate each other to accomplish the mission.

In the hours of painstaking work, the bigger goal had become lost on them but all it took was one reminder to set them on the right path again. In the bright hours of the morning, the team was finally able to fix the prototype and deliver it. It was a testament to the power of people.

I recently sat through a lecture about social justice in my emerging economies class. The professor began by asking us all what justice is and proceeded to spend twenty minutes showing us horrible photos of some of the world's greatest atrocities. These heart-wrenching photos included "The Last Jew in Vinnitsa," the child soldiers in Liberia, Tiananmen Square, and the Khmer Rouge. I don't know exactly what justice is, but that's not it. At the end of the lecture, he told us people often ask him how he is so positive. He looked out at our thirty-person class and said, "You. The world is in your hands."

Dhupar, an engineer who has devoted his life to science and technology, continually emphasizes the value of people. In our efforts to understand the world around us scientifically, we have lost our inherent connection to human power. We have all read the data—in fact, more and more seem to come out every day.

"A truckload of plastic is dumped into the oceans every minute."[172]

"In eighty years, Shanghai, Bangkok, Manila, and Jakarta will be scuba-diving destinations."[173]

These facts should be frightening and almost force you to do something. But if you are anything like me, they likely make you want to curl up into a ball until it goes away. That's because facts like these are overwhelming and, as Dhupar points out, reading the data doesn't allow you to feel the execution and enormous power of people.

> *"When a person is very, very smart or very, very intelligent, they tend to not have faith in the power of humans. They tend to have most faith in the power of processes, systems, and technology, and that is the most important part that most people are missing: that we as a society are not a collection of processes of technology. We as a society are a collection of individuals. We are a collection of people. The moment you lose faith in people, the moment you lose faith in society, is what most people term as practicality, but it unfortunately is the point when you miss out on the magic potential of people coming up with solutions, the magic of the resilience that the people believe."*

In the darkest of times, it wasn't the coding and technology that fixed the prototype. It was the dedicated people who sacrificed their time—and sometimes wellbeing—to ensure

---

172 Robin Hicks, "Be afraid—11 scary facts, stats and lies about our planet this Halloween," Eco- Business, October 31, 2018.

173 Ibid.

these issues had solutions. Each individual there decided to make these sacrifices because they truly believed it was in the interest of the masses. That's how the problem was solved.

Simply put, Dhupar reminds us to "learn from the best, partner with the interesting, and inspire the ordinary."

JUST REMEMBER:

1. Just because it's good does not mean it's easy.

2. Setbacks can be a positive thing because they allow you to tackle bigger obstacles in the future.

3. Focus on the power of people rather than on numbers. When you become overwhelmed with data, remind yourself of the amazing people around the world making a difference. Or better yet, become one of those people.

CHAPTER 7

BEYOND THE PHYSICAL WALLS

——

THE IMPORTANCE OF MINDSET

If you change the way you look at things, the things you look at change.

—WAYNE DYER

For decades, only 10 percent of Philadelphia students have gone on to earn a college degree.[174] More than half of their public schools do not have a college access program and all are generally under-resourced.[175] An overwhelming 75 percent of public school students come from low-income families, most of whom are the first in their family to pursue higher education.[176]

---

174 12PLUS Staff, "The situation," *12PLUS*, Accessed November 24, 2019
175 Ibid.
176 Ibid.

These are the statistics Raymond John encountered when he arrived in Philadelphia.

John grew up with two career options: become a doctor or a lawyer. As the son of Korean immigrants who had spent their entire lives in the United States working at a post office, the culture John grew up in dictated he make his parents proud by becoming something from a preselected list of occupations. When he got into the University of Pennsylvania, he had his chance to make his parent's dreams a reality.

He decided on pre-med because he believed that career path would allow him to help the most people, and so he studied on the pre-medical track in his undergraduate years. After he graduated, he prepared to apply to medical schools but couldn't get himself to send his application in. Instead he took a year to work for a nonprofit in New York.

When he moved back to Philadelphia and began tutoring intercity students with his friend from college, he started examining the school system.

There are numerous after-school programs and nonprofits that work to improve the curriculum at these schools and try to stop the cycles of poverty in the surrounding communities. But as John looked at the history, these programs had existed for decades and so had the statistics. It wasn't that no one was trying to solve the issue, he just felt they were missing something crucial: culture. His nonprofit, 12PLUS, works to change the culture of schools in order to encourage students to pursue post-high school plans.

Within this program, they focus on the environment, the message, and the people. 12PLUS began by building out college/career/academic centers within the high schools and staffing them with recent college graduates who are there during all school hours. The philosophy is simple: The room is more than just a room. Pictures of each student and their accomplishments adorn the walls. The people within foster conversations and help push students to recognize their best selves. Because of this room, 97 percent of the students in their partner schools graduate with a post-secondary plan.[177] This is three times higher than the college matriculation rate of neighboring high schools in Philadelphia and in their partner schools, which was 13 percent.[178]

The physical walls aren't important, but the culture created there is. It works because these students saw their peers graduating and realized it wasn't impossible or out of the norm, but in fact, perfectly possible. When asked, these students all said the same thing: "I thought I would get rejected so what was the point?" Clearly this wasn't the case but all they needed was the encouragement and a change of mindset.

Despite this great accomplishment, John still had to explain why he hadn't enrolled in medical school to his parents. Given his parents don't speak English, he tried to explain his nonprofit organization to them. But in a moment of panic, he could only conjure up the direct translation of "nonprofit": no money.

---

177 12PLUS Staff, Impact" *12PLUS*, Accessed November 24, 2019.
178 Ibid.

* * *

When we envision fighting climate change, we often see it as a physical struggle against greed and companies that pollute the earth, but it has much more to do with the mental. The way we see the world around us and the future greatly impact what actions we take and our influence on others.

Around the time I met John, I was taking an Academically Based Community Service class, in which we taught financial literacy to high school students around Philadelphia. It was a challenging endeavor. When we arrived at our first session, we learned a portion of the class did not speak English and the school lacked a sufficient number of translators for all of the students who needed one. Instead, they relied on bilingual students to translate the entire lesson to the other students while the teacher lectured. The first day we taught, the one bilingual student was out sick. Situations like this are the reality in many public Philadelphia schools.

Halfway through the semester, I learned this school was one of John's 12PLUS schools. I asked to tour the room, expecting a magic space, and found that it looked like all the other classrooms. But here students roamed around asking the facilitators about the Common App, essays, and scholarships. The teachers praised it for helping students with something they never had the time or ability to do. In a school that consistently lacked resources, having a room dedicated to post-secondary plans was a big deal. It showed students that a life after high school was a part of the school the same way the gym and math classes were. Starting their freshman year, these students were now expected to go to college or have other post-secondary plans, so they ended up with fewer absences, higher grades, and a greater ability to see the connections between their classes and future successes.[179]

Culture matters. It mattered in influencing what the students thought was possible in their futures as well as what John thought was possible for his career path. Those around us greatly impact what we consider appropriate or normal. In part, I am writing this book to show you it is all possible because people are doing it. Here is the deal: People are awesome, and the more research I do, and more people I talk to, the less alone I feel with this overwhelming issue.

For the same reason Bah used Facebook to see the inspiring journey of others before becoming his own inspiration, we often need to see others succeed before we can make the leap. Like Bah, you can inspire yourself, but you can also seek out others who make you believe anything is possible and broaden your horizons. You get to choose who you surround yourself with, so choose those who enhance your mindset.

* * *

Angel Wu embodies more of a problem-solving mindset.

I met Wu at a sorority philanthropy event that involved dogs and a frat house. My friend had called out her name and motioned for her to come over before turning to me and exclaiming, "You

---

179 12PLUS Staff, "Our Response," *12PLUS*, Accessed November 24, 2019.

have to meet this girl. She makes things out of leaves." I was intrigued and insisted she get coffee with me.

Wu is a freshman from Canada who is indeed making things out of leaves. She is your typical freshman in college; she is incredibly bubbly as she tells me about figuring out which classes to take, which clubs to apply for, and how to adjust to life away from home.

You would almost never guess she has spent most of her teenage years attempting to redesign the way we consume products.

Wu was a high schooler when she first stumbled upon artist Daan Roosegaarde's TED Talk. In the video, Roosegaarde describes the process of turning smog from Beijing into rings and how he believes "waste from one thing should be food for another."[180] All it took was a twelve-minute video to inspire Wu. She immediately reached out to Roosegaarde to see if she could experiment with the toxic material captured by his smog vacuum. She ran into issues shipping the material, but it did not matter. She was hooked.

That is when she started looking around her and began investigating local sources of pollution. She learned that the EPS (expanded polystyrene) dust produced by packaging manufacturers was ending up in the ocean where salmon and other fish we later consume would eat it. She reached out to the closest manufacturing center to see if she could turn their waste into

---

180 TED, "A smog vacuum cleaner and other magical city designs | Daan Roosegaarde," September 19, 2017, Video, 12:18.

something productive. After two years, she was able to turn this styrofoam waste into molding paste and paint. With the help of her community, she was able to create a final product.

As an artist, she has experimented with turning smog particles into paint pigment. Before arriving at college, she worked with a University of Pennsylvania professor to turn wall paint from major building companies into plastic furniture.

For Wu, innovation never ends. It is not a project but, instead, a continuous way of thinking.

She is constantly reverse-engineering the issues she encounters. When she learned much of the compostable plastic wasn't breaking down properly, she posed a goal: create something that decomposes naturally and as quickly as possible.

During the fall, the colorful leaves begin to envelop the Philadelphia landscape, encroaching on the man-made towers. When the temperatures begin to drop, the leaves fall, covering the streets before disappearing till next spring. It is a beautiful cycle—one we, as humans, have no involvement in. Like many things in nature, what seems like waste recycles itself. Wu noticed this cycle and figured if the things we use are going to end up in the streets, they might as well be made of material that ends up there naturally anyways. That is how she began turning organic waste materials from the city of Philadelphia into packaging material in 2019. Although we already have compostable plastics and other alternatives, Wu learned even these innovations that sound great still take three to five years to decompose and usually end up in places without enough sunlight to allow them to decompose. The paper pulp she is creating out of leaves and other organic materials will make living a sustainable life easier for everyone else.

Wu believes it is up to individuals to show others, especially companies, the solutions. Systems don't change because it is often easier to continue on the same path than to take a risk through changing. In this way, it is up to creative individuals to develop new possibilities for cleaner consumption. This doesn't relinquish responsibility from companies to formulate alternative ideas and become more sustainable. Instead, innovative people can change the landscape and the options available to companies.

"Of course it would be great if everyone could make the change to sustainability, but it's a lot harder to change the minds of a few million. It is much easier to get businesses on board [so] consumers don't have to make a choice."

Ever since I met Wu, I have been immensely impressed with the way her brain works. She never took a break from thinking about solutions and never got tired of it because to her, it wasn't work. "It is not a skill set but a lifestyle," she told me. She explained how even when she does trivial things like brush her teeth, she thinks about the possibilities. "What if it was made from tapioca? How would it feel?"

Yes, there are only twenty-four hours in a day, but if you utilize the capacity of your mind, you can get so much more out of the day. In true innovator form, Wu is always thinking of new possibilities.

* * *

Another huge part of this actionable mindset is positivity.

Isabella O'Brien, a Canadian ocean acidification and lake calcium decline researcher, struggled with the constant influx of negative climate news when she arrived at USC. It wasn't until her teacher suggested the students start every week off with positive environmental news that she was able to deal with her frustrations. Since then, I have also taken up the practice and highly suggest it.

Now every time I hear about horrible storms, I think about how the Italian government introduced mandatory climate change education for all grades, or how Prada just became the first luxury brand to sign a sustainability deal.[181] How China was inspired by the US National Park Service to build a unified park system in order to protect different ecosystems.[182] Or how Sweden has gotten so good at recycling trash they started importing trash to keep their recycling plants going.[183]

We concoct the way we see the world and our beliefs lead to direct changes.

Recently, Sigal Barsade, a professor of management at the University of Pennsylvania, guest lectured my coronavirus class.

181 Jason Horowitz, "Italy's Students Will Get a Lesson in Climate Change. Many Lessons, in Fact," *The New York Times*, November 5, 2019.

182 Christine Larson and Emily Wang, "China aims to build its own Yellowstone on Tibetan plateau," *APNews*, December 3, 2019.

183 Hazel Sheffield, "Sweden's recycling is so revolutionary, the country has run out of rubbish," *Independent*, December 8, 2016.

In her years of research, she has found that fear can make you work harder but not better.[184] If we want people to be able to come up with the creative solutions necessary to solve the global crisis, we need them to be in a good mood.[185] As it turns out, a mild positive mood actually leads to better outcomes.[186]

In one study, doctors given something as simple as a brightly wrapped bag of hard candy were more likely to get the correct diagnosis quicker and less likely to anchor on the wrong diagnosis.[187] This isn't blind optimism—just general positivity and calmness.[188] A positive mood also affects your creativity for the three following days.[189] According to studies on hope versus fear, hope continually trumped fear in entrepreneurial ventures as well.[190] When businesses face adversity and need to decide whether to continue or give up, hope about the future led to greater resilience and the ability to continue working.[191] This state also allows for greater focus, more cooperation, less conflict, and better performance on problem-solving tasks.[192] These are all crucial parts of being able to solve global climate issues. It is also why the culture and mindset we create for ourselves is so important.

184 Sigal G. Barsade, "Emotional Contagion: Epidemics and Human Interactions" (lecture, University of Pennsylvania, Philadelphia, PA, April 22, 2020).
185 Ibid.
186 Ibid.
187 Ibid.
188 Ibid.
189 Ibid.
190 Ibid.
191 Ibid.
192 Ibid.

Negativity is not the only mental barrier to action. As Per Espen Stoknes discusses in his TED Talk, the constant negativity and fear around climate change has led people to set up inner defenses.[193] In his research, he has identified five barriers individuals set up that prevent action: distance, doom, dissonance, denial, and identity.[194] Distance occurs when we hear about negative climate news and imagine it happening somewhere so far away it doesn't affect us.[195] In the last thirty years of climate coverage, over 80 percent of the media has framed it as a disaster, leading to what he calls "apocalypse fatigue": the idea that we are so used to doom we are desensitized to the term's overuse.[196] In the dissonance phase, individuals do not like feeling like hypocrites, so they justify their behavior by pointing to other people's mistakes.[197] In denial, people live and act as if they do not know about the impending doom as a defense mechanism.[198] Lastly, people tend to favor their identities over facts.[199]

In Stoknes' view, most of the problems that surround taking action are rooted in mindset, but then again, so are the solutions.[200] In order to overcome these inner defenses to action, he identified the five S's: social, supportive, simple, signals, and stories.[201] Social refers to how spreading social

---

193 TED, "How to transform apocalypse fatigue into action on global warming," November 17, 2017, Video, 15.

194 Ibid.

195 Ibid.

196 Ibid.

197 Ibid.

198 Ibid.

199 Ibid.

200 Ibid.

201 Ibid.

norms overcome the mental distance we have created.[202] Supportive is reframing the crisis to be about new technology, jobs, and health.[203] Simple references the power of presenting small actions, which make overall action easier.[204] We can overcome denial with signals that help us visualize our progress.[205] Lastly, we can counter identity with stories of the people making a difference.[206]

People are well aware of the facts, so many of the impediments come from our mindset and the mindset of those around us.

Christine Cynn is a documentary filmmaker trying to create stories that change the future. Cynn has spent most of her career making films about political violence, but in 2014, she founded *Hello X*, a story laboratory to imagine the future. Through years of documentary film making, she began to see how the way people remembered the past affected the future. This is when she started experimenting with collective storytelling because, as she emphasized, "It is not a matter of knowing. It is a matter of feeling that you have a responsibility and that you have some agency, that there is something that you can actually do."

In all its storytelling, *Hello X* imagines a young woman fifty years into the future. Anyone can contribute short stories, debate issues with the creative and scientific teams, and suggest

---

202 Ibid.
203 Ibid.
204 Ibid.
205 Ibid.
206 Ibid.

new games. The team created a podcast where they talk to scientists and artists about the future. Cynn has also been working on a mixed reality experience, similar to the Pokémon Go game that will be located in different places around Trumpsa, Norway. In the game, you imagine you are "X" and complete challenges as a biospheric field agent to understand the ecosystems around you. Cynn wants people to be the authors of a collective story, rather than just passively consuming stories.

"I'm also trying to get people to connect [the future] to the decisions that they make every day to stuff that they can actually do; talking to their neighbors, talking to the people who are around them. I think the power that each person has is exponentially more the closer it is to you."

It is a big experiment in seeing if you can change people's mindsets by getting them to consider how their actions impact the future. Cynn believes what you pay attention to grows. So, if you think everything is futile and apocalyptic, you begin walking yourself toward that reality. That is why all of her projects focus on a more desirable future.

"Envisioning it actually creates a possibility. You start walking in that direction just because you're thinking about it—just because you've acknowledged to yourself that you want that."

There is a reason the walls of the 12PLUS schools are littered with signs like "BELIEVE + ACT + INSPIRE."[207] Everything around you influences your reality. Change begins with your mindset, which can ripple out onto others.

---

207 12PLUS Staff, "Our Response," *12PLUS*, Accessed November 24, 2019.

Research shows humans are social creatures who only perform tasks if they think everyone else is doing the same. Studies have shown humans are more likely to take action on anything—not just climate related issues—if they think the majority of people are doing the same.[208] It's social proof—we believe what other people are doing is the right thing to do. In a 2008 study, hotel guests were given two different messages in order to examine which one would get the most people to reuse their towels.[209] The messages all included the same text about saving the planet and facts about the amount of water saved by reusing, but all differed at the end.[210] The two different messages read, "Help save the environment," and "Join your fellow guests in helping to save the environment."[211] The second message also specified that almost 75 percent of guests who were asked to participate in this program did reuse their towels.[212] The first message only caused 35.1 percent of people to reuse their towels, while the second message including the actions of other hotel guests yielded a 44.1 percent towel reuse rate.[213] Even with simple acts such as reusing a towel for one night, calls to action didn't do much unless they were paired with a reference to others who had done the same.

Companies also use this to encourage favorable outcomes. Opower, a software company for utilities, issues reports to its consumers that compare their energy uses to their neighbors

208 Noah Goldstein, Robert B. Cialdini, and Vladas Griskevicius, "A Room with a Viewpoint: Using Social Norms to Motivate Environmental Conservation in Hotels," *Journal of Consumer Research*, March 3, 2008.
209 Ibid.
210 Ibid.
211 Ibid.
212 Ibid.
213 Ibid.

and tips for lowering consumption to the "normal" rate for the neighborhood.[214] According to a study of 600,000 households, these reports have reduced energy consumption by 2 percent overall and 6.3 percent for houses within the highest decile.[215]

And this is a big reason why individual actions matter: because we influence everyone around us. So, when we take action, we change what others consider appropriate and this is how big changes are made.

When humans interact, they create social norms that have a huge effect on the way we conduct ourselves in everyday life. Let's paint a picture:

You are sitting in the window seat of an airplane staring off into first class, wondering what special treatments they are getting up there. But you can't see because of all the smoke wafting through the air. Every once in a while, you cough as smoke fills your lungs. Everybody else does too so it doesn't catch your attention.

Does that airplane scenario sound familiar to you?

Probably not, because as a society we recognized smoking was bad for you and implemented changes. In the 1960s, evidence had begun to suggest smoking cigarettes caused cancer, yet the number of people smoking rose during that seven-year period.[216]

214 Howard Kunreuther and Elke U. Weber, "AIDING DECISION-MAK-ING TO REDUCE THE IMPACTS OF CLIMATE CHANGE," National Bureau of Economic Research, January 2014.

215 Ibid.

216 The New York Times Staff, "Tobacco Industry's Peak Year: 523 Billion Cigarettes Smoked," *The New York Times*, January 1, 1964.

During this time, prices of cigarettes increased as cancer scares became more and more prevalent.[217] In 1963, people in the United States alone smoked 523 billion cigarettes, meaning every person, including children, smoked around 2,764 cigarettes that year.[218] To anyone looking at the situation it probably seemed as though nothing could stop people from smoking.[219]

Back in 1963, you could have looked at the smoking rates and said smoking is truly a worldwide phenomenon that is addictive and somehow transcends cultures in a way little else does. The belief was it will never go away, no matter how many people know it's bad. Looking at the numbers, you could assume it would be impossible to see any change in this habit. But fifty-six years later, we know that is not the case. Knowledge was gathered and shared, laws were implemented, and behaviors eventually changed. Since then, smoking rates in the United States have fallen 67 percent among adults and 68 percent among kids.[220] It is not socially acceptable, or legal, to smoke in public places, airplanes, schools, or around small children. Recognizing there is a problem is step one. That's where we are now with climate understanding.

When I was younger, I would instinctively cough every time I saw someone smoking just to let them know they were hurting themselves and those around them. No one told me to break into public coughing fits and I'm sure it seemed wildly obnoxious, but it goes to show how instinctive norms

---

217 Ibid.
218 Ibid.
219 Ibid.
220 American Lung Association Staff, "Trends in Cigarette Smoking Rates," American Lung Association, March 19, 2020.

are. As a seven-year-old, I felt smoking was wrong because the world around me said so. It was a mindless reaction to someone breaking what I unknowingly saw as a social norm and I reinforced it by being a huge pain and coughing unnecessarily loudly.

Yet again, individual decisions matter in shaping our culture and considerations of what is acceptable.

Because of collective mindset changes, children in Philadelphia's 12PLUS schools are 9.7 times more likely to have post-secondary plans, adults in the United States are 67 percent less likely to smoke, and companies like OPower have reduced energy consumption by up to 6.3 percent.[221] What you believe dictates what you do, and that changes what societies collectively do.

JUST REMEMBER:

1. Your outlook changes your impact. Choose positivity.

2. Our collective mindset influences what we and those around us see as possible.

3. Practice gratitude. Remind yourself of all the beautiful things around you. It will help you stay connected to the world and feel more inspired to save it.

---

221 12PLUS Staff, "The situation," 12PLUS, Accessed November 24, 2019; American Lung Association Staff, "Trends in Cigarette Smoking Rates" American Lung Association, March 19, 2020; Howard Kunreuther and Elke U. Weber, "AIDING DECISION-MAKING TO REDUCE THE IMPACTS OF CLIMATE CHANGE," National Bureau of Economic Research, January 2014.

CHAPTER 8

FAKING IT

——

WHETHER YOU THINK YOU CAN OR CAN'T, YOU'RE RIGHT

Nothing in my house ever quite works. When one of the car windows shattered, we duct-taped a trash bag to the outside. When the oven broke, we duct-taped it shut to cook food. When part of the roof flew away in the middle of a storm, we pretended it didn't happen until it was absolutely imperative to get fixed. So, when the fridge broke my freshman year of college, I was surprised to learn my mom gave up and finally bought a new one.

When I came home from college a few weeks later, my mom showed me the shiny new appliance and exclaimed, "I feel like such an adult!" The woman is married with three kids—from the outside, there is no mistaking her for anything but an adult. As it turns out, even my amazingly capable mom was never given the formula for being an adult.

It is moments like these that remind me that the actions of young people are no less meaningful or important than those of an "adult." I am continuously told by older people, "Age is just a number." There are ages when we are given certain rights like driving, voting, or renting a car, but there are no such requirements or rules for creating change.

When I began looking for people to interview, I searched for young people, usually under thirty, because I believe the most disruptive thinking and fresh perspectives would be evident in young people. I wanted to see the mindset that people my age had employed to make changes, given much of this work will be up to our generation. In doing so, I came across amazing changemakers. But while their youth had given them a new perspective, almost all of them struggled to be taken seriously because of their age.

While there is no better time to make changes than while you're still optimistic and carefree, that attitude doesn't have to end just because other people insist you have to grow up. Unlike Peter Pan, you don't need blind naiveté to hold onto your positivity.

An important aspect of this mindset is believing in yourself and your worth as a changemaker, even when others don't. From what I've seen, convincing others of your vision is an important step in the process and an important quality for success.

There is plenty of advantage in wisdom and experience, which is why mentorship and talking to as many people as possible are critical. But this wisdom becomes an issue when experience is used to diminish new ideas by those with less experience. Ben May, the founder of ThinkOcean and current field organizer for the Joe Biden presidential campaign, has dealt with countless people who didn't understand his vision. His nonprofit connects young environmentalists from around the world in a grassroots network of a hundred chapters in over a dozen countries. There is no shortage of environmental clubs at high schools and colleges but with this network, individuals are able to combine their efforts and create larger-scale changes.

During ThinkOcean's large-scale initiative that led a coalition of its members and partners to spur the passage of a new piece of environmental legislation, Ben and another high school activist were told by a partner who had years of experience in the field that they didn't know what they were talking about how to do it and that their plan wouldn't work. At that moment, they were shocked and called each other after to reassure themselves about the validity of their project and capacity to create change, regardless of age. They took a step back, restored their faith in their coalition's abilities, and moved on. Within a few months, the legislation had been passed. Sometimes experience doesn't mean you know everything.

May told me, "In terms of effectiveness and the capacity to create change, age is not strongly correlated. So, even if you're young—if you're passionate, you have a vision for change, and you have the drive, you can accomplish a lot."

Despite stating the importance of having partners to push their vision forward, he stopped working with partners who see youth-participation as a novelty instead of an asset to their success.

Again, experience is highly valuable but how it is used is the difference between a mentor and an obstacle. Critiques about your vision that help you refine and build a better model are different than dismissing an idea completely and pointing to age and inexperience.

"Listen to critics obviously, but you're inevitably going to be criticized, you're inevitably going to be underestimated, and you should never take it too seriously," said May.

This is not to say this respect does or should come easily. It still needs to be earned. All good changemakers had to be creative to prove they were worth taking seriously and often had to pretend to be changemakers.

When my younger brother was dismissed or ignored by people he reached out to, he convinced his teachers to send out emails on his behalf so the person on the other end could identify an adult. Persistence is key and so are partners.

Anna Luisa Beserra, CEO of Safe Drinking Water for All and inventor of Aqualuz, a way to purify drinking water using the sun, always wanted to be a scientist. When she first began entering contests and developing her product, she was a high school student with no credibility. She struggled to convince people sunlight could disinfect water. But instead of listening to older critics, she just focused on her work until she could prove them wrong. She owes much of her success to this attitude. Her age and inexperience didn't matter because she was able to push through and learn enough to provide clean drinking water to rural areas in Brazil. But it didn't end there and, like many things in life, her positive actions inspired more positive actions.

When Beserra would travel to remote areas that didn't have access to clean drinking water, the people in the area were always incredibly grateful for her services and would always find ways to repay her. In most of these towns, the people didn't have enough for themselves but every time, without fail, they would offer Beserra whatever they had. They offered her food or whatever they produced and invited her to stay the night. They didn't have much, but they wanted to give back.

Climate leaders are in high demand and often those with new ideas or fresh perspectives are just what we need. The actions of leaders go far beyond their lives and those they affect, and they often continue the ripple of positive change. That is why leadership is crucial.

So, without lifetimes of experience, how do we become leaders? As with many things, fake it 'til you make it. It all starts with tricking yourself. As Harvard psychologist Amy Cuddy describes it, if you can approach every situation with more confidence, you create a self-reinforcing model in which you become more confident and others treat you with more respect.[222]

The status enhancement theory states that acting confident and dominant influences others' perception of you.[223] In one study, researchers assigned participants to small groups where they were given a cash prize for answering

---

222 Justin Bariso, "Why 'Fake It Till You Make It' Is So Effective, According to Science," Inc., June 14, 2016.

223 Ilan Shira and Joshua D. Foster, "'Fake It Till You Make It' Turns Out to Be a Good Strategy," Psychology Today, January 2, 2016.

math questions correctly.[224] The members that the groups perceived as more confident were seen as more capable of completing the math problems despite their actual abilities.[225] In fact, researchers later gave feedback on when the group was incorrect, but the other members still perceived the most confident person as the most skilled.[226]

There are other ways to gain experience that don't involve years of your life. As much as people like to pretend they are entirely self-sustaining, every innovator I spoke to mentioned at least one mentor. Many mentors were more experienced people in the field, but some were friends they had met at competitions who understood their passion and drive. For Hugh and Ahmad of Evocco, just having each other made it possible to branch knowledge and experiences as well as share the burden. For Hugh, being young was an advantage. "Age is relative—not just relative to the task but relative to your perception of success. I always associated youth with inexperience, but now I see that youth is a real advantage with no ties or commitments and fueled by 100 percent excitement."

* * *

Lathika Chandra Mouli was twenty-two years old when she started Evergo and won the UN Asia Pacific Low Carbon Lifestyles Challenge.

---

224 Ibid.
225 Ibid.
226 Ibid.

Evergo is a "blockchain-based system which increases proliferation of solar-powered EV charging stations." If it sounds confusing that's because—unless you have a technical background—it is. This became especially evident when Mouli had to pitch her ideas to investors, government workers, and other companies. Being a young woman in a space dominated by older men meant she was often dismissed for being young or not having experience in the clean tech sector. She noticed many of her friends encountered this same issue but, rather than giving in, she found ways to work around the naysayers. When she could tell she had lost the attention of those in a meeting, she would confidently assert herself in the hopes of sounding smarter than the other people in the room. In being confident, she was able to take back power and succeed. The only difference between her successful approach and the times she had been dismissed was her confidence and word choice.

Leadership has nothing to do with age. Being young can be an advantage, which is why there is no better time to change the world than when you're young. Success has much more to do with passion and drive than reaching a certain number of rotations around the sun.

Often, we are our own worst critics. Many of the roadblocks stopping us from going after big things come from within. In middle school, I would often run home and complain about all the work I had, telling my parents it was impossible to do all this work and go to sports practice and still have time to watch The Amazing Race, as we did every Wednesday. It's a common trend I think we all face. I have been complaining since I first learned twenty-four hours isn't as much time as I originally thought. Every time I would tell my dad that middle school, high school, or whatever activity I had embarked on at that time was just too hard, he would look me straight in the face and say, "You know, you're right."

Stunned at how quickly he had agreed with me, I would wait for the part where he told me to keep working or try harder... but he never did. Instead, he would wait just long enough until he saw the look of confusion on my face and say, "As a wise man once said"—a phrase he loves to use when plagiarizing famous people while wanting to let you believe he may also have made it up—"whether you think you can or can't, you're right." And in this case, Henry Ford was right. It has nothing to do with skills—only confidence in yourself.

JUST REMEMBER:

1. Supplement years of experience with mentors in the field and talk to as many people as possible who have advice.

2. Ignore people who dismiss you because of your age. New ideas come from fresh perspectives.

3. Prove credibility with your actions and persistence.

CHAPTER 9

YOU'RE NOT ALONE

AMPLIFYING YOUR VOICE

In 2018, the Kenyan government implemented a nationwide ban on charcoal due to high levels of deforestation. At the time, over 70 percent of Kenyan families used wood charcoal for many of their daily activities, including cooking and heating.[227] This led charcoal sellers to move to neighboring countries, causing huge price spikes many could not afford. Cecil Chikezie was a third-year mechanical engineering student at the University of Nairobi when Kenya banned charcoal. This abrupt decision and its impact on families he knew inspired him to search for a cheaper and more sustainable option. It was not long before he discovered that fuel briquettes made from carbonized agriculture waste were better for the environment and 30 percent cheaper than charcoal briquettes. There were a few individuals who were making these types of briquettes, but they were not able to reach a mass market.

---

227 Daniel Mpala, "Quality of entrepreneurs in Anzisha Prize is up 'tenfold'—initiative's deputy director," *Venture Burn*, November 15, 2019.

While getting his degree, Chikezie started Eco Makaa, an e-commerce company that connects local fuel briquette producers to a client base. Chikezie trains the briquette producers using their standardized formula of carbonized agricultural waste, such as sugarcane residue, as well as discarded charcoal dust. As of October 2019, he had sold more than ten tons of briquettes to 1,100 households and has five full-time and seventeen part-time employees.

But he did not stop there. Chikezie believes words and actions should always go hand in hand. He emphasizes the importance of becoming an outspoken voice for whatever you believe in. Even when he is selling his product, he reminds people of the larger impact. "When we sell 120 kilograms of our briquettes, we are able to save one tree."

His ability to include the community in everything he does is vital to his success as well as the success of larger eco-initiatives. Chikezie believes it is his job as the founder of Eco Makaa to talk about his work. As he sees it, telling other youths about Eco Makaa's impact could inspire them to start their own climate initiatives, which could in turn ripple out into other African countries.

"It becomes a domino effect where we hear stories and we are inspired to start our own thing," Chikezie told me.

When our interview ended, he thanked me for talking to him and allowing him to share these stories. I was utterly confused. Cecil had taken time out of his busy day as a student studying mechanical engineering and running a business. All I had done was bother him until he made time to talk to me about his life. When I hung up, I began thinking about the power of stories. As previously discussed, people everywhere are making important differences in their communities, but we so rarely hear about them. As I will continue to insist, if individuals are going to make a difference in our world, it is vital the contributions from these individuals are elevated and talked about.

A new book by University of Pennsylvania professor Dr. Sarah Jackson and Northeastern University professors Dr. Moya Bailey and Dr. Brooke Foucault Welles entitled *Hashtag Activism: Networks of Race and Gender Justice*, argues that one of the most important ways to spur real change is to "lift up impacted voices."[228] Many people dismiss climate change because they don't see themselves personally affected and wait until it is too late. Not only do people respond more to stories about humans making or implementing change, those most affected have important information and possible solutions that need to be shared. The authors are quick to point out we should be allowing affected people to share their own stories to create more inclusive progress.[229]

It is vital we infuse as many different dialogues and points of view into the conversation as possible. Otherwise, we are stuck with our narrow views of the problem that don't paint a full picture, resulting in solutions that are not always accurate. For example, we might think all plastic straws are evil—until we realize disabled people need them, often to

---

228 Natasha Pinon, "How to ensure your online activism has an offline impact," *Mashable*, December 3, 2019.
229 Ibid.

survive. The world is filled with so much negativity, especially surrounding climate change, that it is more impactful to point out what people can do rather than the structural speed bumps holding them back.

Cecil's story is impressive and unique but even sharing the little things you and those around you are doing can be impactful. My editor, Melody, is always trying to come up with ways to make her life greener. From collecting rainwater during storms to wash her car, to finding local green products, to writing letters to first ladies about ways they can inject green initiatives into their already-existing policies, she has taken many actionable steps to change the world. The difference is, she doesn't stop there. She uses her social media networks to share her progress and ask for more ideas. She has also been able to connect with similar people who have shown her all sorts of environmentally conscious initiatives, from great sustainable clothing and purses to what she should do with the extra rainwater she collects. Turns out you can use it in your toilet as well! She is an eco-innovator just as much as Cecil Chikezie because, at the end of the day, contributing to a better world for yourself and others is what being a changemaker is all about.

* * *

We are often told actions speak louder than words and that holds true. But without amplifying our voices and the voices of those around us, our actions cannot ripple outward. Without talking about the issue and potential solutions, we will continue to live in denial and partisan deadlock and nothing larger will be accomplished.

After Renee Lertzman took her first environmental science class in college, she became so stressed and afraid she almost dropped out of college.[230] She ended up on a field study in California in which she talked openly, for the first time, with the rest of her group about the world and her fears.[231] It was in these moments she began to feel less afraid and thought to herself, *"What if by understanding ourselves and one another, we could find our way through this crisis in a new and different way?"*[232]

Lertzman is now a climate, energy, and environmental psychologist. In her TED Talk on turning climate anxiety into action, she introduces the idea of a window of tolerance.[233] According to Lertzman, every human has a threshold of how much stress they can handle before they disconnect.[234] On one end of this spectrum, people become depressed and on the other end, people succumb to denial.[235] Anywhere outside the window of tolerance, we lose our ability to be resilient, adaptive, integrated problem solvers.[236] She believes the constant negativity of climate change findings may be pushing us out of our windows of tolerance.[237] It is not that facts are bad. However, the way we deal with them is the problem.

It may seem as though people do not care about climate change but, in fact, everyone does. Not everyone has consciously

---

230 TED, "How to turn climate anxiety into action," March 2, 2020, Video, 13:57.
231 Ibid.
232 Ibid.
233 Ibid.
234 Ibid.
235 Ibid.
236 Ibid.
237 Ibid.

connected the dots between climate change and how it affects them. And even if we have, we all just cope with it differently. As Lertzman interviewed people around the world about how they felt regarding the environment, at some point everyone expressed their deep concern for the environment and fear about the future.[238] It had nothing to do with political or ideological belief. Rather, the intense fear pushed many outside of their window of tolerance into denial or depression.[239]

Because of this perceived apathy, many people believe they have to illuminate the facts and motivate people to act, and to some extent, we do need motivation. But this often leads to more numbness and inaction as we become more intimidated by the powerful and daunting statistics.[240]

Lertzman's solution: compassion and becoming more in tune with yourself.[241] It may sound unrelated to the larger issues we are facing but, as she points out, much of this is a psychological issue.[242] From there, it is possible to begin reaching others with the types of honest conversations Lertzman first had during her field study in California.[243]

This is not some feel-good excuse for inaction, but we often forget how much our psychology dictates our response to problems. In fact, a large obstacle to action is the pervasive belief that we are alone in caring about climate change. As Lertzman

---

238 Ibid.
239 Ibid.
240 Ibid.
241 Ibid.
242 Ibid.
243 Ibid.

demonstrated anecdotally, this just is not true. Research by the Yale Program on Climate Change Communication confirms it. According to their April 2019 report, the American public greatly underestimates how many other people believe climate change is happening.[244] The results of the study show Americans think only 54 percent of the general public believes climate change is happening, whereas the actual number is 69 percent.[245] Because humans are such social creatures, these numbers are not insignificant. Those who view the majority of other Americans as climate change believers are more likely to engage in pro-climate behaviors and discuss it with their friends and family.[246] Those who believe the opposite are more likely to self-silence and not discuss climate change.[247] Additionally, one in five Americans "don't know" how many others believe climate change is happening.[248]

Openly discussing the problems we face is an important indicator of our ability to solve these issues. Our incorrect belief that we are the only ones who care only leads to more anxiety and inaction.

The data from the Yale Program also shows that although the majority of people agree climate change is real and will affect future generations, most people don't think it will affect them

244 Anthony Leiserowitz et al., "Climate Change in the American Mind: April 2019," *Yale Program on Climate Communication*, June 27, 2019.

245 Ibid.

246 Ibid.

247 Nathaniel Geiger and Janet K. Swim, "Climate of silence: Pluralistic ignorance as a barrier to climate change discussion," *Journal of Environmental Psychology*, August 21, 2015.

248 Anthony Leiserowitz et al.,"Climate Change in the American Mind: April 2019."

personally and they rarely, if ever, talk about it. That's what led atmospheric scientist Katharine Hayhoe to conclude the single most important thing we as individuals can do to fight climate change is to talk about it. If we don't talk about it, she says, why would we care? And if we don't care, why would we act or support others who do?

Many people see climate change as a giant boulder at the bottom of a hill that only they and a few other people are trying to push to the top, she says. But this is not the case. In her view, the boulder is already starting to roll down the other side of the hill with millions of hands pushing it. The problem is it's just not going fast enough yet. We need more hands.

Hayhoe was studying physics and astronomy when she took a class on climate science and learned climate change was a threat multiplier, making every humanitarian issue the world currently faces worse. She decided this was too important to ignore and, for graduate school, shifted her studies to atmospheric science with a focus on policy-relevant research that would help decision-makers tackle climate change. In addition to her important work helping people around the world quantify the impacts of climate change and create more data, she has made it her mission to make her work more accessible to the public and talk to anyone she can about climate change.

Hayhoe stressed that you have to start from the heart and talk about why climate change matters to us as well as what we can do to fix it. Without these types of conversations, the issue can become divisive or polarized, people tend to get lost in what they view as more pressing priorities, or people do not know how to combat the damages. No matter how personally committed you are, if you believe you are the only one who cares, you will not be able to accomplish much.

> *"The fear and anxiety inherent in the thought that I personally have to fix this problem'...that might take us through a hundred meters, but it's not going to take us to the finish line of a marathon. We're going to burn out way before we get to the end," Hayhoe says. "And climate change is a marathon, but we are all in this together and we all have something different to contribute."*

In Hayhoe's view, rather than altering their diet or travel or changing their lightbulbs, the biggest impact an individual can have is to talk about climate change, join an organization that can amplify voices, and advocate for change at every level—from our families and our schools to our cities and our places of work. This way, changes can be made that are much larger than ourselves. Despite her concern as a scientist, Hayhoe is optimistic and stresses rational hope. This is not blind hope that evolves from denial or ignorance of the situation. Rather, it is hope informed by how disrupted things are. But with recognition, we can make a difference. If there is no hope, there is also no reason to act. She says, "We can't give in to despair. We have to go out and actively look for the hope that we need that will inspire us to act."

The way you look at problems is fundamental to the way you choose to solve them. I recently sent an interesting but depressing article titled "The Decade Tech Lost its Way" to my dad. It listed some of the unfulfilled promises of technology in the early 2000s. The idea that we were possibly moving toward an apocalyptic future scared me, but I nonetheless thought my dad would find it fascinating. Without skipping a beat, he sends back an article entitled, "The 2010s Have Been Amazing." It detailed all the progress made in the last decade. After discussing both articles with him, I was no longer afraid.

The people around you have a profound impact on your worldview and your actions. My dad seems to embody the idea of rational hope and, thankfully, insists on talking me down whenever I get scared about the future. It is with his reminders about the beauty of the world that I am able to remain hopeful and continue moving forward. It is imperative we continue talking to others to remain rational problem-solvers and avoid fear paralysis.

JUST REMEMBER:

1. Talk with your friends and family about why climate change matters and what you personally can do to reduce carbon emissions, prepare for its impacts, and spread the word to and support others.

2. Find an organization that can amplify your voice and impact more people. Ask how you can help.

3. Share hopeful stories of lesser-known climate solutions and innovators making a difference.

BECOME A HUMMINGBIRD

———

IMAGINING A NEW WORLD

In some far-away land, a forest is being consumed by fire. Immediately, all the animals run out from their hiding places and are transfixed by the fire's magnitude. They don't move out of a paralyzing fear for their safety and livelihoods.

Only the hummingbird moves. He begins to fill his tiny beak with water from the nearby stream and flies back and forth from the fire to the stream as fast as he can. Meanwhile, all the bigger animals stand there, helpless, reminding the hummingbird that his actions are futile because he is so small and the fire is so big. Rather than being discouraged, the hummingbird tells them, "I'm doing the best I can," before continuing to put out the fire one drop at a time.

In Wangari Maathai's story, she encourages us to all become the hummingbird.

"I may feel insignificant, but I certainly don't want to be like the other animals watching as the planet goes down the drain. I will be the hummingbird, and I will do the best I can."[249]

Throughout Maathai's lifetime, she has embodied the spirit of the hummingbird. Born in a small village in Kenya, Maathai was always dreaming big. She was educated, which was uncommon for women at the time, and eventually earned a scholarship to attend a university in the United States where she studied biology and later received a master's degree in biological sciences.[250] She returned to Kenya and was the first woman in East Africa to earn a doctoral degree and, later, the first woman in the region to chair a university department at the University of Nairobi.[251]

Against the odds, she received a great education and provided a life for herself, while most others in her community were not so lucky. At the time, rural Kenyan women reported that their streams were drying up, they had to travel farther and farther for firewood, and their food supplies were running low.[252] In 1997, Maathai started the Green Belt Movement, an effort to help both those women and the environment.[253] Her organization paid women to plant trees, which resulted

249 Dirt! The Movie, "I will be a hummingbird - Wangari Maathai (English)," May 11, 2010, Video, 2:00.
250 Biography.com Editors, "Wangari Maathai Biography," *Biography*, July 1, 2019.
251 Ibid.
252 The Green Belt Movement Editors, "Our History," The Green Belt Movement, Accessed May 27, 2020
253 Ibid.

in the planting of more than thirty million trees and 30,000 jobs for women.[254]

Maathai not only provided new opportunities, but she also challenged Kenya's land management and misgovernance. She was arrested and beaten many times for her protests and political efforts. But in 2002, she was appointed assistant minister of environment, natural resources, and wildlife.[255] Just two years later, she was awarded the Nobel Peace Prize for "her contribution to sustainable development, democracy and peace."[256]

In her memoir, Unbowed, she wrote, "What people see as fearlessness is really persistence."[257]

She never stopped being the hummingbird, and rather than ignoring the overwhelming problem, she flew as fast as she could until the fire had been put out.

In her Nobel speech, Maathai said her work, "Challenged the world to broaden the understanding of peace. There can be no peace without equitable development, and there can be no development without sustainable management of the environment in a democratic and peaceful space."[258]

---

254 Biography.com Editors, "Wangari Maathai Biography," *Biography*, July 1, 2019.
255 Ibid.
256 Ibid.
257 Ibid.
258 Ibid.

* * *

As we all stand staring at the fire blazing in front of us, it is crucial we all become hummingbirds.

We have known the climate was changing since 1965 when Lyndon B. Johnson's President Advisory Committee panel warned greenhouse gases were a "real concern."[259] Yet as Former President Barack Obama said, "We are the first generation to feel the impact of climate change and the last generation that can do something about it."[260] This is incredibly frightening, but it also means we will have to start paying attention and addressing the issue head-on. No longer are the days we can wait for governments to take charge. They have had the information for decades and have done very little. We stand at a pivotal point in history, one where our individual actions truly matter for millions of people around the world. But this should not scare us—rather, it should empower us.

Individual people matter because people make up systems. Everything we have accomplished so far as a society we did as people working together toward a common goal. It is naive to think we are now powerless to the systems we created.

Currently, we focus on the things that divide us and the impediments to our goal instead of the success stories all

---

259 BBC Staff, "A brief history of climate change," *BBC News*, September 20, 2013, https://www.bbc.com/news/science-environment-15874560.

260 "Remarks by the President at U.N. Climate Change Summit," *Obama White House Archives*, September 23, 2014, The White House, https://obamawhitehouse.archives.gov/the-press-office/2014/09/23/remarks-president-un-climate-change-summit.

around us and building on the opportunities from climate mitigation.

The changemaker attitude is not blind faith that this problem will fix itself. It is the understanding that we, individually, have the power and opportunity to solve a pressing and disastrous problem. It is knowing that by taking action locally, we can overcome the paralyzing fear. It is avoiding the insignificant fights over trivial matters. It is acknowledging people everywhere who are making a difference. It is recognizing we can personally take action despite not having all the answers. It is understanding everyone encounters setbacks and to use those to gain experience. It is changing our outlooks to influence our actions and the actions of those around us. It is connecting with other people who share our visions and conquering challenges together with our collective knowledge. It is finding ways to use our voices to inform, inspire, and uplift others.

* * *

Humans have faced insurmountable obstacles before, yet we have prevailed time and time again.

The future has always been uncertain, but as I write this quarantining in my childhood home, I am reminded once again how little we know about the future. As scary as that can be, it also gives me hope.

Without a massive disruption, it was unlikely wide-scale changes would be made. While the world is stuck inside, emissions have fallen by 17 percent. Even more than that, we have begun to long for the outdoors in a way our busy lives did not allow.[261] Dolphins and jellyfish swim in the now-clear Venice Canals, wildlife has returned to places humans have taken over like beaches and national parks, and the Himalayas are visible from 125 miles away for the first time in thirty years.[262]

These are not permanent changes, but it does show how the path we were heading down before the pandemic was abnormal. We have deviated so far from normal it took a complete worldwide shutdown to show us what the world is supposed to look like. Returning to normal cannot entail a full economic shutdown with humans stuck in their houses.

So, what should the new normal look like?

From this crisis, I hope we will learn that changing the status quo is possible. We have been given an opportunity to redesign our world. Even as we are battling a deadly virus, we are seeing the environment more integrated into our lives than we thought. A study from the Harvard T.H. Chan School of Public Health recently compared COVID-19 deaths in 3,000 United States cities and found even small increases in long term exposure to pollution led to higher death rates.[263]

While we are living in an extreme situation, we are learning it is possible to fly less and conduct business remotely. I believe

261 Denise Chow, "Carbon emissions dropped 17 percent globally amid coronavirus," *NBC News*, May 19, 2020.

262 Frank Kummer, "7 ways the planet has gotten better since the coronavirus shutdown," *The Philadelphia Inquirer*, April 22, 2020.

263 Lisa Friedman, "New Research Links Air Pollution to Higher Coronavirus Death Rates," *The New York Times*, April 7, 2020.

there is no returning to normal after this. However, I really hope we will be able to question, for the sake of our planet, our prior beliefs on what was considered essential in our lifestyles. We are making extreme sacrifices right now, but we have learned it is possible, even if we hope to never have to make those choices again.

* * *

As a piece from *The Economist* entitled "Seize the Moment: The Chance to Flatten the Climate Curve" pointed out, we are currently in a unique position to force political change and enact policies at a lower social and political cost than would have existed before.[264] As the world enters a new period of change, we can demand society catch up. For the first time, we can design a world that is looking forward to not simply avoiding devastating consequences but creating benefits from potential hardships.

This is a world that maximizes opportunities around green jobs and sustainable companies. One that prioritizes humans and the environment and puts a price on negative externalities. A new world built with people *and* the environment in mind.

We used to see this utopian world existing in novels or a future so far off it probably took place on Mars, but now that all visions of the near future have been wiped away, why not create the society we want now? This world does not shift blame from polluting corporations to individuals but rather

264 Andrea Ucini, "Countries should seize the moment to flatten the climate curve," *The Economist*, May 21, 2020, 13.

makes individual and corporate eco-friendly decisions easy. The false dichotomy between the environment and the economy disappears as policymakers think beyond their short office terms and consider a sustainable future.

None of this is a given. We are enduring an unprecedented crisis with real human costs. Once the dust settles, there will be urgency to return to normal. But how beneficial was that normal really?

It is time to get loud. To work together. To be innovative. There is no time for pessimism. No time to dismiss the hummingbird for its petite size. We need brave leaders.

None of this will exist unless people can loudly demonstrate the value of a different vision for the future. Pre-pandemic, we could tell ourselves continuing down this path was inevitable.

"It is how it has always been done."

"Destroying an entire system and rebuilding is difficult."

But that excuse no longer exists. Those systems were not sustainable. Let's make something that is.

Be a mighty hummingbird.

APPENDIX

———

INTRODUCTION

Griffin, Paul. "CDP Carbon Majors Report 2017." The Carbon Majors Database, CDP. July 2017. https://b8f65cb373b1b7b15fe-b-c70d8ead6ced550b4d987d7c03fcdd1d.ssl.cf3.rackcdn.com/cms/reports/documents/000/002/327/original/Carbon-Majors-Report-2017.pdf.

Kahn, Matthew E., Kamiar Mohaddes, Ryan N.C. Ng, M. Hashem Pesaran, Mehdi Raissi, and Jui-Chung Yang. "Long-Term Macroeconomic Effects of Climate Change: A Cross-Country Analysis." The National Bureau of Economic Research. NBER Working Paper No. 26167 (2019). http://papers.nber.org/tmp/7281-w26167.pdf.

Marlon, Jennifer R., Brittany Bloodhart, Matthew T. Ballew, Justin Rolfe-Redding, Connie Roser-Renouf, Anthony Leiserowitz, and Edward Maibach. "How Hope and Doubt Affect Climate Change Mobilization." Frontiers in Communication. 4, 2297 (2019): 1-5. https://www.frontiersin.org/article/10.3389/fcomm.2019.00020.

Sky News Staff. "What Will Happen As The World Gets Warmer?" Sky News. October 8, 2018. https://news.sky.com/story/what-will-happen-as-the-world-gets-warmer-10336299.

Wei, Yi-Ming, Rong Han, Ce Wang, Biying Yu, Qiao-Mei Liang, Xiao Chen Yuan, Junjie Chang, Qingyu Zhao, Hua Liao, Baojun Tang, Jinyue Yan, Lijing Cheng, and Zili Yang. "Self-preservation strategy for approaching global warming targets in the post-Paris Agreement era." Nature Communications. 11, 1624 (2020): 1-4. https://www.nature.com/articles/s41467-020-15453-z.

CHAPTER 1

Andrews, Eve. "Climate anxiety doesn't have to ruin your life. Here's how to manage it." Grist, September 5, 2017. https://grist.org/article/how-i-learned-to-stop-worrying-and-deal-with-climate-change/.

Clayton, Susan, Christie Manning, Kirra Krygsman, and Meighen Speiser. "MENTAL HEALTH AND OUR CHANGING CLIMATE: IMPACTS, IMPLICATIONS, AND GUIDANCE." March 2017. https://www.apa.org/news/press/releases/2017/03/mental-health-climate.pdf.

Ford, Brett Q., Phoebe Lam, Oliver P. John, and Iris B. Mauss. "The psychological health benefits of accepting negative emotions and thoughts: Laboratory, diary, and longitudinal evidence." Journal of Personality and Social Psychology. July 13, 2017. https://doi.org/10.1037/pspp0000157.

Hardin, Garrett. "Tragedy of the Commons." The Library of Economics and Liberty. Accessed April 30, 2020. https://www.econlib.org/library/Enc/TragedyoftheCommons.html.

Huizen, Jennifer. "What to know about eco-anxiety." Medical News Today. December 19, 2019. https://www.medicalnewstoday.com/articles/327354.

Leiserowitz, Anthony, Edward Maibach, Seth Rosenthal, John Kotcher, Matthew Ballew, Matthew Goldberg, and Abel Gustafson. "Climate Change in the American Mind: December 2018." January 22, 2019. https://climatecommunication.yale.edu/publications/climate-change-in-the-american-mind-december-2018/2/.

Style Like U. "How Terminal Cancer Showed Beth Fairchild That She Was Enough." Facebook. October 2019. https://www.facebook.com/stylelikeu/videos/446066302932214/?v=446066302932214.

CHAPTER 2

Franklin, Benjamin. "Poor Richard's Almanack, 1737." AMDOCS: DOCUMENTS FOR THE STUDY OF AMERICAN HISTORY. Accessed April 20, 2020.

Haworth, Sacha. Twitter post. July 15, 2019. 11:39 a.m. https://twitter.com/sachalouise/status/1150822204524912646.

Houck, Brenna. "Why the World Is Hating on Plastic Straws Right Now." Eater, July 12, 2018. https://www.eater.com/2018/7/12/17555880/plastic-straws-environment-pollution-banned-alternatives-ocean-sea-turtle-viral-video.

Ho, Vivian. "'People need them': The trouble with the movement to ban plastic straws." The Guardian. August 25, 2018. https://www.theguardian.com/us-news/2018/aug/25/plastic-straw-ban-california-people-with-disabilities.

McGrath, Jane. "Which is more environmentally friendly: paper or plastic?" How Stuff Works. August 20, 2008. https://science.howstuffworks.com/environmental/green-science/paper-plastic1.htm.

PR Newswire. "Responding to Trump's Plastic Straws, Bernie Sanders Supporters Launch "Trump Sucks" Metal Straws." Market Insider. August 5, 2019. https://markets.businessinsider.com/news/stocks/responding-to-trump-s-plastic-straws-bernie-sanders-supporters-launch-trump-sucks-metal-straws-1028416609.

Rainey, James. "How business groups are fighting a wave of anti-plastic straw laws." NBC News. March 1, 2019. https://www.nbcnews.com/news/us-news/how-business-groups-are-fighting-wave-anti-plastic-straw-laws-n977196.

Rainey, James. "'Banning plastic straws will not be enough': The fight to clean the oceans." NBC News. December 30, 2018. https://www.nbcnews.com/news/us-news/banning-plastic-straws-will-not-be-enough-fight-clean-oceans-n951141.

Rosenbaum, Sophia. "She Recorded That Heartbreaking Turtle Video. Here's What She Wants Companies Like Starbucks to Know About Plastic Straws." Time, July 17, 2018. https://time.com/5339037/turtle-video-plastic-straw-ban/.

Seattle City Council. "Plastic Bag Ban." Seattle.gov. Accessed April 20, 2020. https://www.seattle.gov/council/meet-the-council/mike-obrien/plasticc-bag-ban.

Swim, Janet, Susan Clayton, Thomas Doherty, Robert Gifford, George Howard, Joseph Reser, Paul Stern, and Elke Weber. "Psychology and global climate change: Addressing a multi-faceted phenomenon and set of challenges." American Psychological Association 66. (August 2009) 241-250. https://www.apa.org/science/about/publications/climate-change-booklet.pdf.

Taylor, Jessica. "Trump Seizes On Soggy Paper Straws As Campaign Issue: 'Make Straws Great Again'." NPR, July 19, 2019. https://www.npr.org/2019/07/19/743683131/trump-seizes-on-soggy-paper-straws-as-campaign-issue-make-straws-great-again.

Warren, Elizabeth. Twitter post. September 4, 2019. 8:58 p.m. https://twitter.com/ewarren/status/1169444615612764160.

Zdanowicz, Christina. "A man attacked a McDonald's employee over a straw and she fought back." CNN, January 4, 2019. https://www.cnn.com/2019/01/02/us/customer-attacks-mc-donalds-employee/index.html.

Zeitlin, Matthew. "Do plastic bag taxes or bans curb waste? 400 cities and states tried it out." Vox Media. August 27, 2019. https://www.vox.com/the-highlight/2019/8/20/20806651/plastic-bag-ban-straw-ban-tax.

CHAPTER 3

Biography.com Editors. "Rosa Parks Biography." *Biography.* April 24, 2020. https://www.biography.com/activist/rosa-parks.

Brzezinski, Ginny. "How Shannon Watts went from stay-at-home mom to founder of the largest gun violence prevention org in the U.S." *NBC News,* March 4, 2020. https://www.nbcnews.com/know-your-value/feature/how-shannon-watts-went-stay-home-mom-founder-largest-gun-ncna1149651.

Editorial Staff. "Effectiveness of Mothers Against Drunk Driving." *Alcohol.org.* March 30, 2020. https://www.alcohol.org/teens/mothers-against-drunk-driving/.

History.com Editors. "'I Have a Dream' Speech." *History.* January 15, 2020. https://www.history.com/topics/civil-rights-movement/i-have-a-dream-speech.

History.com Editors. "Martin Luther King, Jr. born." *History.* January 15, 2020. https://www.history.com/this-day-in-history/martin-luther-king-jr-born.

Hochschild, Adam. *King Leopold's Ghost: A Story of Greed, Terror, and Heroism in Colonial Africa.* New York: Mariner Books. 1998.

Koger, Susan, Kerry E. Leslie, and Erica D. Hayes. "Climate Change: Psychological Solutions and Strategies for Change." *ResearchGate.* December 2011. https://www.researchgate.net/publication/270835783_Climate_Change_Psychological_Solutions_and_Strategies_for_Change.

McLeod, Saul. "Solomon Asch—Conformity Experiment." Simple Psychology. December 28, 2018. https://www.simplypsychology.org/asch-conformity.html.

National Institute on Deafness and other Communication Disorders Staff.

"Podcast Interview with Geraldine Dietz Fox, Patient Advocate." National Institute on Deafness and other Communication Disorders. July 11, 2019. https://www.nidcd.nih.gov/about/history/geraldine-dietz-fox/interview'-dr-geraldine-dietz-fox.

O'Connell, Caitlin. "15 Ordinary People Who Changed History." Reader's Digest. Accessed May 3, 2020. https://www.rd.com/true-stories/inspiring/inspiring-stories-9-ordinary-people-who-changed-history/.

Popova, Maria. "Elevator Groupthink: An Ingenious 1962 Psychology Experiment in Conformity." Brain Pickings. Accessed May 4, 2020. https://www.brainpickings.org/2012/01/13/asch-elevator-experiment/.

Psychology Today Staff. "Bystander Effect." Psychology Today. Accessed May 4, 2020. https://www.psychologytoday.com/ie/basics/bystander-effect.

Simon, Bob. "How a slap sparked Tunisia's revolution." CBS News. February 22, 2011. https://www.cbsnews.com/news/how-a-slap-sparked-tunisias-revolution-22-02-2011/.

TEDx. "The success of nonviolent civil resistance: Erica Chenoweth at TEDxBoulder." November 4, 2013. Video. 12:33. https://www.youtube.com/watch?v=YJSehRlU34w.

CHAPTER 4

Abbasi, Daniel R. "Americans and Climate Change: Closing the Gap Between Science and Action." Yale School of Forestry and Environmental Studies. 2005. https://grist.files.wordpress.com/2006/05/americans_and_climate_change.pdf.

Bashaw, Edward, and Stephen Grant. "Exploring the Distinctive Nature of Work Commitments: Their Relationships with Personal Characteristics, Job Performance, and Propensity to Leave." Journal of Personal Selling and Sales Management. October 2013. https://www.researchgate.net/publication/261572836_Exploring_the_Distinctive_Nature_of_Work_Commitments_Their_Relationships_with_Personal_Characteristics_Job_Performance_and_Propensity_to_Leave.

Ben and Jerry's Staff. "Issues We Care About." Ben and Jerry's. Accessed May 4, 2020. https://www.benjerry.com/values/issues-we-care-about.

Evocco Staff. "About." Accessed May 24, 2020. https://www.evocco.com/about.

Irfan, Umair. "How Delhi became the most polluted city on earth." Vox Media. November 25, 2017. https://www.vox.com/energy-and-environment/2017/11/22/16666808/india-air-pollution-new-delhi.

Kennedy, John. "Evocco teaches consumers how to be sustainable shoppers." Silicon Republic. November 12, 2018. https://www.siliconrepublic.com/start-ups/evocco-sustainable-shopping-app.

Parimukh Staff. "About Us." Parimukh. Accessed March 22, 2020. http://parimukhinnovations.com/#Inno.

Quote Investigator Staff. "Jump Off the Cliff and Build Your Wings on the Way Down." Quote Investigator. October 30, 2015. https://quoteinvestigator.com/2012/06/17/cliff-wings/.

Raz, Guy. March 22, 2020. "Ben & Jerry's: Ben Cohen And Jerry Greenfield (2017)." Podcast audio. How I Built This. NPR. Accessed April 26, 2020. https://www.npr.org/2020/03/20/818918341/ben-jerrys-ben-cohen-and-jerry-greenfield.

Shpancer, Noam. "Overcoming Fear: The Only Way Out is Through." Psychology Today. September 20, 2020.https://www.psychologytoday.com/us/blog/insight-therapy/201009/overcoming-fear-the-only-way-out-is-through.

Taibi, Catherine. "9 Reasons To Love Ben & Jerry's That Have Nothing To Do With Ice Cream." HuffPost. August 15, 2013. https://www.huffpost.com/entry/ben-and-jerrys-love_n_3726083.

CHAPTER 5

Forbes, Moira. "Inside Samantha Power's Hard-Won Wisdom on Inspiring Action." Forbes. July 7, 2016. https://www.forbes.com/sites/moiraforbes/2016/07/07/samantha-powers-hard-won-wisdom-on-inspiring-action/#5dc29e375e40.

Power, Samantha. The Education of an Idealist: A Memoir. New York City: Dey Street Books, 2019.

Slovic, Paul. "Psychic Numbing and Genocide." American Psychological Association. November 2007. https://www.apa.org/science/about/psa/2007/11/slovic.

Small, Deborah, George Loewenstein, and Paul Slovic. "Sympathy and callousness: The impact of deliberative thought on donations to identifiable and statistical victims." Science Direct. July 7, 2005. https://www.sciencedirect.com/science/article/abs/pii/S0749597806000057.

TED. "Ink made of air pollution | Anirudh Sharma." February 8, 2013. Video. 8:24. https://www.youtube.com/watch?v=Dig_QFPPPtE.

TEDx. "The power of the individual | Jennifer Beckner | TEDxMSU." April 15, 2016. Video. 7:52. https://www.youtube.com/watch?v=1VZwj2OVSPY.

Yulman, Nick, and Zakiya Gibbons. February 20, 2019. "Unnatural Resources." Podcast audio. Just The Beginning. Accessed December 22, 2019. https://www.stitcher.com/podcast/just-the-beginning-2/e/58912115?autoplay=true.

CHAPTER 6

Business Standard Staff. "Air pollution kills 1.2 mn Indians in a year, third biggest cause of death." Business Standard. April 3, 2019. https://www.business-standard.com/article/current-affairs/air-pollution-kills-1-2-mn-indians-in-a-year-third-biggest-cause-of-death-119040300300_1.html.

Hicks, Robin. "Be afraid—11 scary facts, stats and lies about our planet this Halloween." Eco-Business. October 31, 2018. https://www.eco-business.com/news/be-afraid11-scary-facts-stats-and-lies-about-our-planet-this-halloween/.

O'Brien, Isabella. "Aquatic Osteoporosis - Remediating the emerging environmental problem of lake calcium decline." March 22, 2017. Video, 3:54. https://www.youtube.com/watch?v=idI-5mlBTERM.

Roosengaarde, Daan. "Projects." Studio Roosegaarde. Accessed January 4, 2019. https://www.studioroosegaarde.net/projects.

TED. "A smog vacuum cleaner and other magical city designs | Daan Roosegaarde." September 19, 2017, Video. 12:18. https://www.youtube.com/watch?v=eVFYhbHpfqU

CHAPTER 7

12PLUS Staff. "Impact." 12PLUS. Accessed November 24, 2019. https://www.12plus.org/impact.

12PLUS Staff. "Our Response." 12PLUS. Accessed November 24, 2019. https://www.12plus.org/response.

12PLUS Staff. "The situation." 12PLUS. Accessed November 24, 2019. https://www.12plus.org/thesituation.

`American Lung Association Staff. "Trends in Cigarette Smoking Rates." American Lung Association. March 19, 2020. https://www.lung.org/research/trends-in-lung-disease/tobacco-trends-brief/overall-tobacco-trends

Barsade, Sigal G. "Emotional Contagion: Epidemics and Human Interactions." (Lecture. University of Pennsylvania. Philadelphia, PA. April 22, 2020).

Goldstein, Noah, Robert B. Cialdini, and Vladas Griskevicius. "A Room with a Viewpoint: Using Social Norms to Motivate Environmental Conservation in Hotels." Journal of Consumer Research, March 3, 2008. https://assets.csom.umn.edu/assets/118359.pdf.

Horowitz, Jason. "Italy's Students Will Get a Lesson in Climate Change. Many Lessons, in Fact." The New York Times. November 5, 2019. https://www.nytimes.com/2019/11/05/world/europe/italy-schools-climate-change.html; Barr, Sabrina. "Prada becomes first luxury brand to sign sustainability deal." MSN Lifestyle. July 11, 2019. https://www.msn.com/en-nz/lifestyle/style/prada-becomes-first-luxury-brand-to-sign-sustainability-deal/ar-AAJXYxR.

Kunreuther, Howard, and Elke U. Weber. "AIDING DECISION-MAKING TO REDUCE THE IMPACTS OF CLIMATE CHANGE." National Bureau of Economic Research. January 2014.

Larson, Christine, and Emily Wang. "China aims to build its own Yellowstone on Tibetan plateau." APNews. December 3, 2019. https://apnews.com/4e11f8b7eab546d692673008ccc90487.

The New York Times Staff. "Tobacco Industry's Peak Year: 523 Billion Cigarettes Smoked." The New York Times. January 1, 1964. https://www.nytimes.com/1964/01/01/archives/tobacco-industrys-peak-year-523-billion-cigarettes-smoked.html.

Sheffield, Hazel. "Sweden's recycling is so revolutionary, the country has run out of rubbish." Independent. December 8, 2016. https://www.independent.co.uk/environment/sweden-s-recycling-is-so-revolutionary-the-country-has-run-out-of-rubbish-a7462976.html.

TED. "A smog vacuum cleaner and other magical city designs | Daan Roosegaarde." September 19, 2017. Video. 12:18. https://www.youtube.com/watch?v=eVFYhbHpfqU.

TED. "How to transform apocalypse fatigue into action on global warming." November 17, 2017. Video. 15. https://www.ted.com/talks/per_espen_stoknes_how_to_transform_apocalypse_fatigue_into_action_on_global_warming/up-next?language=en.

CHAPTER 8

Bariso, Justin. "Why 'Fake It Till You Make It' Is So Effective, According to Science." Inc. June 14, 2016. https://www.inc.com/emily-canal/coronavirus-financial-crisis-advice-for-founders-birchbox-twilio-funding-hiring.html.

Shira, Ilan, and Joshua D. Foster. "'Fake It Till You Make It' Turns Out to Be a Good Strategy." Psychology Today. January 2, 2016. https://www.psychologytoday.com/us/blog/the-narcissus-in-all-us/201601/fake-it-till-you-make-it-turns-out-be-good-strategy.

CHAPTER 9

Geiger, Nathaniel, and Janet K. Swim. "Climate of Silence: Pluralistic ignorance as a barrier to climate change discussion."

Journal of Environmental Psychology. August 21, 2015. https://doi.org/10.1016/j.jenvp.2016.05.002.

Leiserowitz, Anthony, Edward Maibach, Seth Rosenthal, John Kotcher, Parrish Bergquist, Matthew Ballew, Matthew Goldberg, and Abel Gustafson. "Climate Change in the American Mind: April 2019." Yale Program on Climate Communication. June 27, 2019. https://climatecommunication.yale.edu/publications/climate-change-in-the-american-mind-april-2019/.

Mpala, Daniel. "Quality of entrepreneurs in Anzisha Prize is up 'tenfold'—initiative's deputy director." Venture Burn. November 15, 2019. https://ventureburn.com/2019/11/anzisha-prize-entrepreneur-quality/.

Pinon, Natasha. "How to ensure your online activism has an offline impact." Mashable. December 3, 2019. https://mashable.com/article/activism-on-social-media/.

TED. "How to turn climate anxiety into action." March 2, 2020. Video. 13:57.

CONCLUSION

BBC Staff, "A brief history of climate change," BBC News, September 20, 2013, https://www.bbc.com/news/science-environment-15874560.

Biography.com Editors. "Wangari Maathai Biography." Biography. July 1, 2019. https://www.biography.com/activist/wangari-maathai.

Chow, Denise. "Carbon emissions dropped 17 percent globally amid coronavirus." NBC News. May 19, 2020. https://www.nbcnews.com/science/environment/carbon-emissions-dropped-17-percent-globally-amid-coronavirus-n1210331.

Compology Staff. "Our Company." Compology. Accessed May 27, 2020. https://compology.com/about-us/our-company/.

Dirt! The Movie. "I will be a hummingbird—Wangari Maathai (English)." May 11, 2010. Video, 2:00. https://www.youtube.com/watch?v=IGMW6YWjMxw.

Friedman, Lisa. "New Research Links Air Pollution to Higher Coronavirus Death Rates." The New York Times. April 7, 2020. https://www.nytimes.com/2020/04/07/climate/air-pollution-coronavirus-covid.html.

Kummer, Frank. "7 ways the planet has gotten better since the coronavirus shutdown." The Philadelphia Inquirer. April 22, 2020. https://www.inquirer.com/science/climate/earthday-coronavirus-philadelphia-wildlife-pollution-climate-change-20200422.html.

Orts, Eric and Joanne Spigonardo. "No Time to Waste: Achieving the UN's Sustainability Goals." Initiative for Global Environmental Leadership. March 2020. http://d1c25a6gwz7q5e.cloudfront.net/reports/2020-02-28-IGEL-SDG-report.pdf.

"Remarks by the President at U.N. Climate Change Summit." Obama White House Archives. September 23, 2014. The White House. https://obamawhitehouse.archives.gov/the-press-office/2014/09/23/remarks-president-un-climate-change-summit

The Green Belt Movement Editors. "Our History." The Green Belt
    Movement. Accessed May 27, 2020. http://www.greenbelt-
    movement.org/who-we-are/our-history.

Ucini, Andrea. "Countries should seize the moment to flatten the
    climate curve." The Economist. May 21, 2020.

ACKNOWLEDGMENTS

I never imagined myself writing a book and certainly would not have gotten to this point without the support of incredible people. I've discovered, along my journey writing *The Changemaker Attitude*, that publishing a book takes a village and I am so grateful for all of the encouragement. Throughout all the moments of doubt and uncertainty, these people pushed me to keep working and accomplish my goal.

First and foremost, I would like to thank my family for supporting me through every step of the way.

Thank you to everyone who pre-ordered the e-book, paperback, and multiple copies to make publishing possible, spread the word about *The Changemaker Attitude* to gather amazing momentum, and helped me publish a book I am proud of. I am sincerely grateful for all of your help:

Aaron Diamond-Reivich
Abby Baggini
Alex Hazen
Allen Family

Amanda Oh
Beatrice Karp
Beth Wille
Caroline Riise

Carter Cheo
Dalia Vardy
Dano Major
Emily Lawson
Eric Koester
Eric Zimmerman
Erin Hutt
Georgia Ray
Geraldine Fox
Grace Lamont
Grace Lamont
Greg Poshman
Griff Ryan
Gunhild Kristin Jordan
Harry Fox
Jane Kampner
Jennifer Fox
Jessica Niblo
Kim Pantages
Lathika Chandra Mouli
Laurel Henderson
Lauren Fritzinger
Lexi Howe
Liam Rigney
Lily Zirlin
Linda Atkinson
Lisa Haisfield
Lisa McGuire
Lorrain Kramer
Mackenzie Lukas
Margo Ellis
Marni Bond

Mary Chao
Max Traynor
Meghan Lacey
Meghan Moran
Mia Barkenbush
Mikayla Golub
Molly Scharlin Ben-Hamoo
Natalie Turner
Owen Ramberg
Parker Jones
Patricia Atkinson
Peter Westcott
Rachel Saur
Rae Lampe
Randi Dorman
Ricky Wojcik
Robin and Michael Fox
Sam Simon
Samuel Oshay
Sarah Scharlin Ben-Hamoo
Sarah Ward
Scott Kendrick
Serena Miniter
Sherri Smith
Simone Lamont
Sofy Maxman
The Leibinger Family
The Seeman Family
The Seltzer Family
Trevor Fedyna
Zibby Schwartz

To the people who took time out of their lives to be interviewed, I cannot thank you enough for talking to me and for making a difference in the world.

Ahmad Mu'azzam	Cecil Chikezie
Alhaji Siraj Bah	Christine Cynn
Amber Sparks	Emily Hazelwood
Amit Singh	Hugh Weldon
Andreas Gruson	Isabella O'Brien
Angel Wu	Jack Fox
Anna Luisa Beserra	Jay Koh
Arpit Dhupar	Katherine Hayhoe
Ben May	Lathika Chandra Mouli

Lastly, a huge thank you to New Degree Press, especially Eric Koester, Melody Delgado Lorbeer, Brian Bies, and Natalie Bailey, for supporting and encouraging me along this journey.

Made in United States
Orlando, FL
22 January 2023

28929091R00085